Kay Collier-Slone

SINGLE
in the
CHURCH

*New ways to
minister with 52%
of God's people*

An Alban Institute Publication

The Publications Program of The Alban Institute is assisted by a grant from Trinity Church, New York City.

Library of Congress Catalog Card Number 92-72459
ISBN #1-56699-058-0

To those who share the solo flight,
especially to the memory of Lucy Stanley,
whose written words helped give us all wings.

CONTENTS

Sunday morning is church time. A certain rhythm belongs to the early hours of the first day of the week. It is both expectation and habit. On the occasional Sunday morning when for some reason or other I am out and about in the world during these church-time hours, I experience a revelation. A whole "other" society is out there, going about its business. A whole other way of being; a different rhythm of life.

So, too, the revelation of being "suddenly single" at age forty-five.

A counterculture exists about which I, and apparently others, had no inkling. It is a different rhythm to adult life as previously experienced. But it has its own rhythms, its own norms, and an increasing number of people who are a part of it.

As a journalist I specialize in investigating psychosocial and religious issues. During my years of doctoral studies in counseling psychology, subspecialties in divorce recovery and life transitions put me regularly in touch with singles of all ages and led me to the pioneer field of singleness for further study.

The further I have explored as journalist, counselor, and teacher, the more I have found to probe and understand. I've discovered that whether one comes to singleness as a young adult, middle adult, or older adult, my church, and many other churches as well, have little to offer in terms of a theology of humanity that embraces singleness; little understanding of crises particular to singleness; no help to offer in exploring the meaning of single life, especially in relation to issues of sexuality, accountability, and social concerns; no concept of inclusiveness in program and leadership; no understanding and teaching of being single, of living single in a coupled world. And no awareness that these issues have profound connections with major areas of concern in both sacred and secular society.

For the past five years, I have been involved in the ground-breaking work of ministry to single adults in both the secular and religious worlds, as private and group counselor, psychosocial journalist-lecturer-consultant, and coordinator of singles' ministry within an Episcopal diocese and cathedral.

I have talked with hundreds of singles of all ages and walks of life. I have listened to their stories and shared their joys, sorrows, and frustrations. I have found myself in the unlikely and unsought position of advocate for "single rights."

My own singleness provides gut-level validity to research. Singles are in the peculiar position of living in a new paradigm, while society, both sacred and secular, stubbornly clings to the old. Moving toward a new century, we who live in the reality of this new paradigm must speak out with forthrightness, must move out of the shadows and into the light so that those around us may see and hear that neither the rhythm of singleness nor the rhythm of coupled is *better*—only *different*. Then together may we move toward accepting and embracing that difference as essential and life-giving to the wholeness of the family of God.

Kay Collier-Slone
Lexington, Kentucky
1992

ACKNOWLEDGMENTS

This book is more phenomenological and heuristic study—experiential reflection and response that has grown out of my life and work as a single person—than quantitative scientific research. For the excitement and credibility of the science of phenomenology and heuristics that gain such work a place in research, I am indebted to Clark E. Moustakis, Ph.D., of the Center for Humanistic Studies in Detroit and to Bruce Douglass, Ph.D., of the Union Graduate School.

I would like to express my deepest thanks to many single individuals—whether they have become known to me through workshops, conferences, letters, telephone calls or personal visits—for their courage, honesty, directness, sense of humor, hard work, determination, loving hearts, and especially for trusting me with their precious and life-giving stories.

To the staff and participants in Solo Flight One. To all the members of Christ Church Cathedral and Diocese of Lexington Intergenerational Ministries to Single Adults.

To Lucy Stanley, whose words in the article "Ministry to Single Adults?" written in *The Advocate*, touched a responsive chord in single Episcopalians across the country and helped give wings to this work.

To all those leaders who willingly told the stories of their experiences in ministry to single adults and who give of themselves daily in this pioneer work.

To the Rt. Rev. Don A. Wimberly, Bishop of the Episcopal Diocese of Lexington, Kentucky, and the Very Rev. James L. Burns, Dean of Christ Church Cathedral, Lexington, for their strong and loving support of the concept and work of single-adult ministry.

To Wendy Winkler, who typed and retyped, in the midst of great personal stress.

And to those clergy and singles whose request for this material and questions about when they could have it in hand assured that it had to be.

Every effort has been made to ensure that proper credit has been given to those whose words, written and spoken, have been quoted here and whose ideas are part of the fabric of this book. Should there be any unintentional omission, it will be noted in future editions.

CHAPTER I

Singles Speak: Who Are We?

Sunday morning at Saint Mark's

Looking down from the pulpit, the Rev. Peter Curtis's eyes scan the congregation. More and more these days, individuals arrive alone and often sit alone. Early in his ministry, he looked out on more family groupings; any single individuals were scattered and often elderly.

Who are these people Father Curtis has noticed, and how do we account for this change in demographics?

You see, Peter Curtis and Saint Mark's Church are not alone in experiencing demographic change. The huge increase in the number and proportion of people living alone in the United States has influenced membership trends in all denominations.

Dr. Kirk Hadaway, the United Church of Christ secretary of research and evaluation, points out the net result of this trend: Denominations are slowly becoming less family-dominated, with a need for "all denominations to increase their emphasis on providing ministry to persons who are in non-traditional families."[1]

"They were once the exception," says Hadaway. "Now they are the rule. This expanding segment of the population is critical to the future of the church."

Names and Faces

These "non-traditional family units" have names and faces—and exist in congregations large and small—in virtually every denomination.

RANDY, forty-one, is an executive for a large corporation. He has chosen never to marry—for a variety of reasons: being busy with a career that required frequent travel; enjoying occasional dates but never feeling that "the right person emerged at the right time." Randy lives in a sprawling, professionally decorated home built to suit the lifestyle he would like to maintain if his company would leave him in the area long enough. A life-long Episcopalian, he joined a parish shortly after moving to the city. He attends regularly and has made a few attempts at Sunday school and church dinners but hasn't found a way to feel particularly connected. "I seem to be a fish out of water," he comments. "Most of the people who seem near my age are involved with families, with couples."

SARAH, twenty-nine, is a young professional who grew up in her Presbyterian parish and has come back to her home town to establish herself professionally after living out of state during her college and graduate-school years. She has a network of friends and acquaintances developed over the years, a number of whom have married and are starting families. Sarah knows that she is a part of a grouping new to both church and society and feels pressured by both. "No one seems to think that a person is grown up until they are married," she says. "I am an adult, with adult responsibilities; I have lived on my own for seven years now, not counting college. I do not see marriage in the immediate future. People just don't get married as early as they once did. My generation needs to know how to take care of itself, whether we marry or whether we don't marry. Women in my age group by and large expect to do that. Looking around at the marriages failing, including that of my parents, I know that I would rather remain single than be married to the wrong person. As such, I may be well into my thirties before I seriously consider marriage. And, somewhere down the road, if the right person doesn't come along, I may just invest my savings in a house and a sperm donor and get on with my life. I come to church here fairly regularly, and I see a few faces my age in the congregation. I wish there were a way to meet other people like me. Sometimes I don't say a lot about church to other people, but I would like to know more about the Bible, to look at issues in my life from a faith perspective . . . but I don't know whether I would be judged or what."

HARRY, forty-seven, has been divorced for three years—his choice. His wife and children no longer attend his parish, where they were all active for many years. Harry continues in leadership roles and is primarily involved in the same social and professional circles in which he was involved prior to the divorce. He has a busy social calendar; hostesses count on him as the "extra man" to escort single friends and relatives for dinner parties. "My life is comfortable here," he says. "It always has been."

PATTIE, thirty-six, is also divorced "by choice," choice born of necessity. She has finally left an emotionally abusive marriage and with her two elementary-school children is beginning life anew in a new community where she is a legal secretary at an established firm. "My life is nonstop," she says. "Kids, work, house, kids, work, house. It is a major struggle to get to church on Sunday morning. I am too tired to move, and it's hard to get the kids going. It's also really hard to figure out the time, much less the money, to get them involved in anything beyond the basics. I'm exhausted all the time. I don't like to leave the kids alone too much, even if I could afford a sitter, which I can't. My life has changed pretty dramatically. If we had made this move as an intact family, even a dysfunctional one, we would have had two salaries and there would have at least been another adult in the house. Then there would have been time and money to do volunteer activities, to get into the kind of things where friendships can develop. I'm getting to know the mothers of some of my children's friends, but I'm not expecting that to be a great source of friendship or social life. I'm one more extra woman in a society that has too many of them already. I stay busy with the kids and their activities, mostly. They are with their dad for some vacations, and two months in the summer. That's really lonely."

JOYCE, fifty-nine, has never married. She is a professor at the university and has renovated a duplex in a settled area of the city within easy commuting distance of the university and downtown. She is a regal, striking woman whose leadership skills are sought by both the university and the community. She has been attending this large, downtown Lutheran church for fifteen years. "I have a good salary, and I contribute proportionately," she says. "In the past five years, I have begun to be a little restless about the perspective here. It is *very* family oriented.

While I don't mind contributing to the youth-group van, I'm obviously never going to have a child to use that van. I would like to see a portion of the money go to work for single people of all ages, not just my money but the church's money. After all, I'm a 'family unit' also!"

JESSICA, sixty-seven, has left a financially disastrous marriage after forty-five years. While her resources are extremely limited, she is feeling the freedom of knowing the truth concerning her own financial affairs. She has found part-time work as assistant to the owner of a large real estate firm where she is earning minimum wage. She also house sits and does alterations to pay for her tiny efficiency apartment. She has been active in the Episcopal church all her life and is aware that she no longer has the time or resources to participate as she once did. "Truthfully, I'm happier in many ways than I've been in years and years," she says. "But I *am* awfully tired just trying to hold body and soul together and well aware that the last of my 'good' clothes are wearing out, that I don't have the money to replace them, and that I just don't have the strength or energy to do altar guild or that kind of thing."

TERRY, thirty-three, has been separated from her husband for ten months. A tall, slender, athletic brunette, she and her preschool children cling to one another and to her parents who also attend the midsized parish in which they have been active for many years. Terry had taught school immediately after college, married at twenty-eight, and now has a three-year-old and a sixteen-month-old. She appears dazed. Her parents seem equally troubled. Terry is facing decisions regarding return to the work force, decisions that will require her to take some refresher courses before she can get on the waiting list for a teaching position. Her parents are on fixed-income retirement and live in a small apartment. "There are so many problems, I'm not sure which way to turn first," she admits, tears never far from her eyes. "I was going to go back to work in a few years, but I wasn't prepared for this *now*. His payments to me are not consistent, and the actual divorce process is just beginning. I just want it over, so I'll *know*, but everyone keeps telling me not to hurry or I'll be sorry. My mom isn't really well enough to help me with the children on a long-term basis, and I know they don't have any extra money, although they really try to help. Father M— has been helpful and has even helped me get some counseling. But I'm scared. Actually, I'm terrified, and I cry a lot."

SISTER MARY HELEN, seventy-one, is in charge of a regional urban nursing mission and regularly attends a large downtown church. Generally several other sisters reside at the mission as well. Sister Mary Helen is very active in the religious community of the city and is a popular retreat leader and speaker. Few people give thought to a nun's personal network. Sister Mary Helen says, "My closest friends are really the few single clergy around here and a single woman or two. We really enjoy talking, laughing, and just having some relaxed time. I don't say much more about it to anyone . . . They might get the wrong idea."

CAROL, forty-nine, has been divorced for eleven years. Her oldest child has recently married; her youngest has just started college. Although divorced for many years, she is just looking at the issue of being truly alone in her home for the first time. "I thought I was lonely before—busy, overworked—but kids were in and out. We did the usual church things. Now with the last one out of the house, I am beginning to realize there are some things I've yet to learn—really some grief and anger I've delayed facing, although not intentionally. It is just so *lonely* when I get home from work at night. And Sunday afternoons are interminable!"

JIM, thirty-six, is a doctoral student in psychology. He moves like the college athlete he once was; his dark sandy beard gives him a slightly professorial air. He lives alone and attends services at the large Episcopal church in his city. He serves occasionally as an usher and has been on several diocesan and parish committees. Jim is gay. His lifestyle, if known, is not acknowledged or discussed.

KEVIN, fifty-one, is a divorced clergyman with joint custody of his three teenage children. "Our marriage just didn't work anymore," he says. "Nothing horrible—just a slow death. She finally had the courage to say it was over and moved out. We're still friends. It's been five years now, so I'm pretty well established in singleness. But I know that my career in the church may be destined to be the kind of interim work I'm doing now. And I can't imagine what life will be like when the kids are gone for good."

SUSAN, thirty-eight, is a widow. Her husband was killed two years ago in an automobile accident. It was a second marriage for both. His daughters live in another city with their mother. They adore Susan, but their time with her is very limited these days. They will soon be going to college. Susan's home is in another state, but she has been teaching in this community since her husband was transferred here. His parents are out of state as well. Susan is comfortable in her home and work, but church and social life have dwindled after the initial surge of sympathy and support. She feels she should be "recovered," but "I still find it awfully hard."

HAROLD, sixty-eight, is a widower who recently retired as a professor. "It is so lonely," he says. "I do all of the things people tell you to do. I volunteer. I play golf. I talk to my grown children. I do a little consulting on the side. I've gotten a dog. I really don't want to sell the house, but it's been four years now and I just don't know. 'Dating' doesn't seem the right thing for me at my age. But I want female companionship. Not marriage, necessarily . . . I'm not sure I'll ever want to marry again. But I miss female talk. And I don't want people thinking I'm a dirty old man, so I just don't talk about this to anyone."

LOUISE, thirty-nine, and NANCY, forty-two, are single mothers who have established a home together with their children from early marriages. Louise is an accountant; Nancy is an attorney. They consider themselves committed to each other for life, although neither the church nor the state gives official recognition to their lesbian relationship. To protect the security of their jobs, and their children, they present themselves to the world at large, and to the church where they are all quite active, as single women.

MARTHA, forty-three, has been divorced for thirteen years. She considers herself well established in singleness. Early in her single life, she had two long-term relationships. She has not been involved in a relationship now for about six years. Occasionally she has a dinner date or goes out on business. She has a busy professional life and a busy personal life. "I've been lucky. I have a few really good friends . . . one couple that doesn't just stick to other couples when they're entertaining, and one good male friend. My life is very busy and very full."

KELLY, twenty-seven, is a young professional who has remained in her home town to pursue her career. She is single, by definition, but hates the term. "I don't consider myself 'single,'" she says adamantly. "I'm just me. I don't want anything to do with anything that has a 'single' label on it. I have plenty of friends. I have plenty to do. My job is coming along okay. I'll get married if I choose to, or not get married, as the case may be."

The list goes on:

A thirty-year-old social worker who has recently moved from out of state; never married.

A fifty-one-year-old interior decorator, divorced two years, in counseling again after her ex-husband's remarriage.

A fifty-six-year-old only son, recently widowed, with a mother in a nursing home six hundred miles away.

And on and on . . .

Myth versus Reality

A close look at singles and their lifestyles will shatter many of the myths that stereotype unmarried adults.

Randy, Sarah, Pattie, and Jessica are "voluntary singles." They have chosen their particular state of singleness.

MYTH: The choice of singleness—choosing never to marry or being the person to leave a marriage—removes the element of grief and pain.

REALITY: The choice of singleness—deciding never to marry or being the person to leave a relationship—may *lessen* the element of pain or cause the grief and pain to occur at a different time in the process than the pain of the involuntary single. But the pain of making even a necessary decision to leave a marriage or not to marry may involve the death of dreams and expectations of lifestyle. It may also involve the judgment of family, friends, church, and society.

MYTH: People who choose the single state do not experience loneliness, do not have a high need for inclusion or socializing.

REALITY: While *some* who choose singleness may be particularly well suited by personality or conditioning to the single lifestyle, this does not preclude the need for friends and companionship or the battle of loneliness.

Terry, Carol, Kevin, Susan, Harold, and Elizabeth are "involuntary singles"—people who did not desire or choose divorce or widowhood but had it thrust upon them.

MYTH: Divorced or widowed people who are lonely and/or unhappy have simply not worked through their grieving or anger and gotten on with their lives. They could be happy if they would just pick up and move on.

REALITY: Divorced and widowed people do need to go through a process of recovering from grief and loss. The length of time required to go through this process differs for every person. Part of this process will involve adjusting to major changes in their lives, their friends, their worlds, which may be unanticipated but real. Lives cannot simply be "picked up where they left off." The divorced or widowed person may, even post recovery, still have to face change and pain that resurfaces. This does not necessarily point to dysfunction or unwillingness to "get on with life."

MYTH: Singles live a glamorous, hedonistic lifestyle.

REALITY: The "swinging single" is a stereotype that exists primarily in movies and books. The majority of single individuals live the kinds of lives described on previous pages—ordinary, routine, daily lives. Singles' bars are not the normal hangout for the majority of single people.

MYTH: Single is neither a normal nor desirable way to live.

REALITY: Today nearly one-half of the U.S. adult population above the age of twenty-five is single. Numerically, the state of singleness is a new norm in this country, although not widely recognized as such. Single is neither better nor worse than coupled or married—simply different.

MYTH: The grief of the death of a spouse is worse/easier than the grief of divorce.

REALITY: While the two kinds of loss have much in common, there are also differences in the grieving. Again it is important to note that it is not a matter of which is more or less. Both losses involve pain and grief that require time, understanding, and, often, assistance to recover.

MYTH: Divorce is so commonplace these days that everyone adjusts easily.

REALITY: Divorce is not a circumstance where frequency lessens pain. Each person, each couple, each family still has to experience its particular and specific divorce. Research indicating that divorce is a common occurrence in this society does not lessen its impact.

MYTH: Never-married singles do not feel marginalized or alienated as divorced or widowed singles do because they are not dealing with grief or bitterness.

REALITY: Never-married singles have their own painful issues and do experience feelings of alienation, loneliness, and marginalization. They are often less understood than any category of single persons because they are perceived as not having followed the accepted "norm" of marriage, and they are not parents; in short, neither church nor society knows what to do with or for them. This category of single people sometimes can also be ignored from within the single community as efforts to deal with recovery issues overshadow the very real needs of the never-marrieds.

MYTH: *Single* is essentially an incomplete or broken state, and those who are single are bereft.

REALITY: Singleness in itself is neither incomplete nor broken nor sad. It is simply one of several states of being.

MYTH: *Single* is (1) a transitional state between childhood and marriage; (2) the ongoing state of a small minority of the population on the periphery of life; or (3) life's terminal state.

REALITY: *Single* is one of several optional, normal states available to adults in today's society. There may be several "seasons of singleness" in a person's life, i.e., after high school or college, midlife, or late life single-again.

Why the Shift?

Why has this shift occurred in our society and churches? Why do pastors look into congregations with more single members today than in previous times? Is this a trend that is likely to continue?

1. In 1983 the average age for marriage in the United States was eighteen to twenty-three. In 1991 the average age for marriage was twenty-seven-and-a-half.

Reasons? There are more acceptable options for young people today in terms of travel, professions, and housing. This generation is also the first to reach its twenties with two probabilities: First, many of its number will be divorced at least once. Second, it will take American households two incomes to sustain a comfortable style of living in the twenty-first century. Consequently, the twenty-somethings to thirty-somethings are taking the time to live on their own and develop inde-pendence and security prior to marriage. Many are questioning the viability of the institution of marriage itself and considering other options. Live-in arrangements, single-parent adoptions, sperm-donor babies, group-housing arrangements are all becoming norms—acceptable options to early marriage or marriage per se. Fewer than twenty-seven percent of the households in the United States today consist of mother, father, and children.

2. The fastest-growing age group in the country is eighty plus. Futurists predict that by the year 2000 there will be one hundred thousand people over the age of one hundred. Forty percent of the adults in this country are already over the age of sixty-five. Many in this age group are single, primarily women. The postretirement group is physically and mentally younger than ever before and able to live more productive lives. Yet the realities of loss of pension and social security through remarriage and lack of understanding of normal needs for companionship are problematic for senior singles. Many in this age group are not likely to identify themselves as "single," still psychologically and spiritually experiencing themselves as "married."

3. Divorce rates remain steady. With no-fault divorce prevalent throughout the country and the stigma attached to divorce all but gone in an immediate sense, no downward trend is expected. The number of people single-again through divorce appears to have leveled off and be holding firm.

Old Paradigms and New

In the past the church has related to single people theologically, pastorally, psychologically, educationally, and personally within the context of a definition of family that, like some gigantic computer, tossed out any case—including single people—it was not programmed to understand and process. As a result of this lack of understanding, there has been no recognition of the fact that there is, indeed, a difference in issues of singleness nor has there been any movement toward specific trained ministry to work in this area.

It would be unthinkable for any church to have no youth ministry budget. There is a staff position for youth ministry when at all possible. At the very least, ministry to youth is a regular part of the program of every parish.

Why?

Because children exist, and their particular needs exist and will continue to exist as a normal part of life in our society. The needs of youth are the same as adults in terms of (a) needing and wanting a loving, accepting church family and (b) needing and wanting spiritual nurture. The needs of youth are different from the needs of adults in some program areas, however. People with children will not be interested in a church unless it has a good youth program that speaks to a young person's needs.

The same rationale applies to ministry for single adults. Singles exist; their particular needs exist, and they will continue to exist. The time is long past when any church can view the individual cases of the Harrys, Patties, Randys, and Carols in the congregation as being "outside the norm," to be dealt with only case by case. It is time for a theology of humanity that includes seasons of singleness as a normal part of the life span. The forty-eight percent of the adult population of this country that is single today spends its Sunday mornings both inside and outside the church doors. Some are singles in the pews of churches not equipped to understand or assist in their lives. Many more are outside the church door, not attracted to even stage one of basic church laity because they do not feel welcome.

If youth ministry makes one statement, it loudly and clearly says "we know you exist" to a large segment of the population with special, as well as universal, needs.

Lack of ministry to single adults is denial of a large and ever-growing segment of the population.

It is painful to have one's very existence denied or ignored. The church, like society in general, has based its programming, its resources, on a marriage model. As author Carolyn Koons points out in her ground-breaking book *Single Adult Passages: Uncharted Territory,* even developmental psychology is based on marriage as a norm. When people fall off these developmental charts through divorce or widowhood, the efforts of society are to get them back on the charts, remarried as soon as possible, so that everyone is "comfortable" again.[2]

Speaking to a group of Protestant pastors, Koons, a never-married professor of human development at Azusa Pacific University, said, ". . . and if someone *never* marries, and therefore has never gotten *on* the charts, people *really* don't know what to do with them."[3]

Church programming and budgeting has focused on the married and familied. The concept of nuclear family has been elevated to icon. Author Janet Fishburn speaks to this in her book *Confronting the Idolatry of Family: A New Vision for the Household of God.*

Fishburn points out that as organizations and individuals speak of changes that have taken place in family and society, they have often turned to the 1950s as the desired model: the time remembered with nostalgia and longing, the time when family seemed sacrosanct, the world safe, and things not so "out of control." This line of thinking tends to blame the sixties for all that is perceived wrong with the world —the time when things got off track and the new liberal standards started society on a downward slide.

Fishburn recommends a look at the entire spectrum of modern history, which shows what she calls "a steady pace" from the Victorian period until World War II. What appeared to be a sudden change in national moral values was not discontinuous with developments in American culture since the beginning of the twentieth century. The

Victorian code taught and sustained in Protestant churches became un-
workable in the culture at large, according to Fishburn. The so-called
sexual revolution of the sixties was not "an explosion of over-sexed
youth" nor the seemingly "sudden disregard of family life as a sign of the
end of family." Both events signaled "the end of the power of the Victorian sexual ethos to inspire protestants to live according to Victorian
values."

Fishburn continues by saying that church members and leaders who
came of age before or during the years of national optimism and economic expansion that followed World War II have a vision of the way
the world ought to be. That vision symbolizes that time when all was
well with the world again. America had triumphed over the powers of
evil. Families were reunited. So-called "normal" family life resumed.
The fifties saw the basic element of the American Dream recovered with
a compelling force: family stability, a rising standard of living, seemingly unlimited career opportunities. Any person who came of age in a
small town in postwar America experienced the kind of homogeneity that
no longer exists.[4]

The reemergence of the Victorian family ideal was, according to
sociologists and historians, "the last spark, a temporary spark of a dying
ethos."[5] The fifties were but one decade of apparent calm and "apple
pie" life in America when a norm was established; against that norm a
world appeared to go crazy in the sixties. Had the fifties not happened,
the events of the sixties would not have seemed so shocking, so out of
sync. Since the end of World War I Americans have been acquiring a
more urbane flavor that did not mix well with the Victorian moral code.
The sixties only made more obvious the changes that had already taken
place. The decades that followed were only phases in a much longer
cultural transition in which the stated ideals and moral codes of the
Victorian era were gradually being discarded.[6]

For the purposes of this study, it is important to realize that it pleases
most of society to believe that we live in the old paradigm, not the new.
Singles, however, know the paradigm shift has occurred. They live in
that new paradigm.

CHAPTER II

Build It, and They Will Come: Where Ministry to Single Adults Is Working

"Build it, and they will come."

The words, from the movie *Field of Dreams,* speak of a baseball field to be built on a farm and of athletes who will play there and fans who will be drawn to the unlikely spot: a cornfield in Iowa. In real life people touched by the dream in that movie still drive to the film site in Iowa as if to touch a symbol of hope and faith. "Build it, and they will come."

The Rev. Chuck Treadwell quoted those words, referring to singles' ministry and the parish church. For those who have long been working for this ministry to develop, the words carry a *Field of Dreams* full-bodied hope and faith.

Where a church has a ministry to single adults, it has come from the impetus—and the deep conviction—of an individual, clergy or lay, and an emerging constituency. Those efforts that appear most organized and have experienced the greatest longevity are *institutionalized*; they have become a part of the program and budget of a church; they receive priority treatment. Such programs most often exist in large parishes. In smaller parishes the efforts toward ministry to single adults may not be as immediately obvious; it may not take the form of particular groups or events, but exist more in attitude and theology.

When discussions of ministry to single adults arise, someone invariably asks the question "What is singles' ministry?"

The complex answer can best be understood by reading the stories of those parishes where ministry to single adults is thriving. This chapter tells the stories of single-adult ministries in several congregations. The stories are organized by factors that impacted the ministries' start up and evolution. At the conclusion of the chapter, we'll point out similarities and differences in the ministries and universal messages to be learned from the models.

We will consider six factors of the various ministries:

Factor 1. A senior pastor who detected an area of ministry in need of attention.

Factor 2. A staff person with special training, experience, and ability in the field.

Factor 3. A plan for financing the ministry.

Factor 4. Determination of priorities in the program.

Factor 5. A mission statement and flexibility around that statement.

Factor 6. Ongoing evaluation and adjustment.

Single-Adult Ministry at Saint Michael and All Angels Episcopal Church in Dallas

Factor 1. A senior pastor who detected an area of ministry in need of attention.

The ministry to single adults at Saint Michael and All Angels was instituted by the Rev. Bob Ratelle, a senior pastor who saw a growing need in his city and among parishioners of Saint Michael, one of the largest Episcopal churches in the United States. Ratelle determined to hire a staff member to work with this single population, an estimated forty-seven percent of the adult population in the ten zip codes in which most of Saint Michael's parishioners lived; sixty percent of these single adults had never been married.

Factor 2. A staff person with special training, experience, and ability in the field.

The Rev. Tom Blackmon was hired by Saint Michael in the spring of 1984 with the specific assignment of developing a comprehensive ministry to single adults. Prior to this assignment, Blackmon had been on the staff of Saint Alban's Church in Washington, D.C., where he had shepherded a significant number of parishioners through the divorce process and had been involved with a parish day-care center that had worked with both male and female custodial parents. These *pastoral experiences* gave him working knowledge of aspects of single life that needed to be addressed by the church.

Blackmon had another significant credential for this work. He was divorced himself.

Blackmon, who remarried early in 1992, is aware that the question of single or married leadership for singles' ministry is "arguable" in some circles. Yet he has no doubts about the importance of the single-adult experience as a credential for working with singles' ministry.

"I feel as though an effective single-adult leader will have experienced adult singleness for at least five or six years somewhere along the road," he says. "It may be postcollege, premarriage; it may be five or six years midlife-single-again. If you have not had this experience, it is hard to connect with the feelings. You don't hear certain things; don't feel certain emotions. You don't know to the core the feeling of loneliness, the need to build a sense of family. That comes through living as a single adult."

Factor 3. A plan for financing the ministry.

Saint Michael and All Angels is a parish of just under six thousand communicants. Approximately forty percent, or some two thousand of the adults over the age of twenty-two, are single. The median age of the parish is thirty-four.

Saint Michael is not an endowed parish. It has a unique history of starting innovative programs by soliciting one or two specially designated pledges over a three-year period; these are gradually supplemented by the operating budget, finally to be absorbed by that budget. Both the Christian education and youth programs of the parish were started in this manner. Singles' ministry would follow the same pattern.

But the bottom dropped out of the Texas economy shortly after Blackmon's arrival; fantasies about a number of new programs died. Fortunately, pledges of $25,000 over a three-year period were solicited, supplemented by $15,000 to $20,000 from the operating budget. Today, single-adult ministries has a $50,000 share of the church's operating budget, exclusive of the salaries of Blackmon, his two assistants, and a part-time secretary. Blackmon acknowledges that he could "responsibly use" an additional $25,000.

In a 1987 Plan for Ministry, the singles' council listed five reasons their parish should invest in ministry to single adults:

1. To better correlate parish priorities and programs with the population of the parish. Theologically speaking, we need to do a better job of feeding the sheep who happen to be in our flock.

2. To give us the program "weapons" we need to successfully evangelize single people in north Dallas, helping this parish maintain its "cutting edge" of new, open, energetic, and productive members.

3. To increase the stewardship of time, talent, and treasure of new and old single parishioners, thereby returning to the parish what it is investing by expanding this ministry over the next three years. We believe that the increased pledges of money and talent will put this ministry "in the black" within three years.

4. Offer a uniquely Episcopalian approach to singles' ministry that works carefully to integrate and not segregate people and attends to the program principles outlined above. [See appendix 3.]

5. Finally, as one of the largest Episcopal churches in the nation, we should be pioneers in moving our church at all levels to focus resources and energy on ministry to single people. We need to prod and lead our church from little interest in this ministry to an interest more in tune with the human reality of our culture.

Factor 4. Determination of priorities in the program.

Blackmon met with singles in the parish shortly after his arrival in Dallas. Based on his observations and conversations, he decided his first priority had to be to begin to deal with the divorced population—in particular, single parents. "They were angry," says Blackmon. "They had felt marginalized over the years—excluded in language and leadership. They had to come first. The second priority group was singles under the age of thirty-five. At that time parish statistics showed 2,100 singles between the ages of twenty-two and seventy-five; 343 single parents. Statistics from The Alban Institute show that between fifty-five and sixty-five percent of the under thirty-five population is unchurched.

Blackmon also felt that he needed additional information from successful singles' ministries to help him establish the program at Saint Michael. During the first year of his tenure in Dallas, he spent time exploring single-adult programs in the Southwest, Pacific Northwest, and West Coast areas, picking the brains of Presbyterians, Methodists, Roman Catholics, and staff and parishioners of free churches and evangelical churches.

He developed a three-point plan:

1. Start with the perceived needs of the congregation. (Single parents, divorced, young singles.)

2. Offer a balance of social outreach, spirituality, recovery, and educational activities.

3. Try to build a sense of family.

Factor 5. A mission statement and flexibility around that statement.

The mission statement developed by Saint Michael and All Angels began in a discussion of single parish lay leaders and singles' staff on what single people need from the church and what they have to offer. The purpose statement was developed through many drafts in a four-month planning process. It reflects what the team learned as they progressed through significant changes. It is guided, the singles' council says, by "our theological self-understanding," which includes four affirmations:

1. We all need God.

2. We all need each other.

3. God is revealed to us as we live in community and serve one another.

4. As we live and serve, we all have much to learn about giving

and about receiving. Ministry of, by, and to single people at Saint Michael is therefore intended to:

a. Affirm and enrich our lives as spiritual persons through opportunities for worship, learning, service, recreation, and mutual support.
b. Create and nurture opportunities for growth and relaxation that are healthy, honest, and respectful of our diversity (that is, as to gender, marital history, economic status, etc.).
c. Encourage an atmosphere of belonging and acceptance that acknowledges us as single persons, and, at the same time, enables us to be more fully integrated into the life of the parish as a whole.
d. Open new avenues for sharing the special gifts that single people consistently bring to church life—innovativeness, enthusiasm, staying power, flexibility, creative use of our time.

With these purposes in mind, the Saint Michael's ministry began with programs to meet the immediate needs.

Two groups for single parents emerged—one for those with young children; one for those with adolescents. As in the majority of programs, age lines were not firmly drawn but were self-selecting, along interest lines, having to do with life rhythms.

Blackmon instituted a divorce-recovery program in which a twelve-week seminar evolves into an ongoing support group for those recently divorced. The seminar is built around a death and resurrection theme. "Dying, rising," says Blackmon, "and passing through hell in between." With the help of local clinicians and other clergy, Blackmon leads the opening sessions and the concluding ones by helping participants look at critical issues. A seminar might include:

Starting Over after Your Divorce

Session 1: Can Grief Be Good?

Session 2: Grieving through Divorce

Session 3: Coping with Stress and Getting On

Session 4: Getting to Know Yourself and Where You're From

Session 5: Rebuilding Self-Esteem

Session 6: Money and Lifestyle

Session 7: Socializing, Dating, and Boundaries

Session 8: What Is Emotional Intimacy?

Session 9: Morality and Sexuality

Session 10: Looking Ahead—Evaluation and Goal Setting

Session 11: Socializing and Dating

Session 12: Summing Up

All of the clinicians involved in the presentations have been or are single adults. When he feels it necessary, Blackmon refers people to specific counseling programs beyond the parameters of the seminar. For those who feel a need for further support, the seminar evolves into support groups. Blackmon is also prepared to offer the Sacrament of Reconciliation (confession and absolution) "when a person is spiritually and emotionally ready to let go."

The burgeoning number of young singles called for the establishment of a group that became known as Young Singles. The midlife singles included a large number in need of the divorce recovery ministry, as well as those who were simply hungry for a unit within the church where they could feel a sense of identity and comfort. A social outreach group for the thirty-five to fifty-five age group was established under the name Singles' Discovery.

Factor 6. Ongoing evaluation and adjustment.

At the conclusion of year one, self-evaluation showed group cohesiveness to be at a high point. Group members felt a desire to reach out to others through service projects.

By the end of year three, Blackmon began assembling a team to assist in the growing ministry. As a midlife single, he felt it important to have a leader who, by age and interest, was more in touch with the young single population. The Rev. Chuck Treadwell, a recent seminary graduate who had lived for five years as a never-married single, was hired for this post. Treadwell feels he brings to his job an understanding of the pressures of early career, which is the life focus of this age group, and firsthand knowledge of what it is to be on his own and alone in a new place.

In assembling the team, Blackmon looked at his own skills in envisioning, administering, empowering, teaching, and ministering in crisis and recovery. These abilities were balanced by Treadwell's youth and gregarious and extroverted abilities with people, and the abilities in spiritual direction, spiritual formation, and pastoral care of lay leader Kimberly Rogers. They are assisted by a part-time secretary three days per week.

Blackmon is adamant about staying away from the "guru thing" he feels has sometimes been crippling in youth ministry.

The singles' ministry department decided at this point in its growth to bring in a consultant to assist in the ongoing evaluation of needs and setting of long-term goals. [See worksheets and plan as developed in appendix 3.] With the consultant, they determined what they wanted to accomplish in four major areas: (1) personal and spiritual growth; (2) identity; (3) outreach; (4) social activity.

In the area of inreach, or personal and spiritual growth, Sunday school classes are offered for singles. One is based on the lectionary; the other is issue oriented. Recent topics have included The Sacrament of Healing, The Eucharist—Its History and Theology, Other Offices of *The Book of Common Prayer*, What Kind of King?, Resurrection Power, and Sexuality and Responsibility.

The Tuesday evening supper-fellowship-worship format developed by Young Singles has grown into an every-Tuesday-night program for three different singles' groups—younger, middle, more mature—with all of the groups gathered on a quarterly basis for a supper-speaker evening. Sample Tuesday night topics have included Religion and Politics in the Middle East; the film *Shadowlands*, which chronicles the life of C. S. Lewis; speakers from the community in areas of sports, cultural, or political life; speakers on pertinent church issues.

In the area of identity, the shepherding committee takes care of special needs such as cards and flowers to singles who are sick or hospitalized. The hospitality and welcome committee is on a constant lookout for newcomers, to bring them fully into the Saint Michael's community and inform them of what is available to them through the singles' programs.

Single parents have activities they share with their children, such as Easter egg dying, craft days, kite flying, and picnics. The church also offers parents adult-only activities, such as pot luck suppers at homes or evenings at local restaurants.

The outreach area involves singles in monthly activities, such as a party for an "adopted" nursing home, working on a Shared Housing building project in the Dallas area, and being available as resources to an adopted case worker for the Department of Human Resources. Singles volunteer their expertise as dentists, lawyers, hairdressers, doctors, teachers, and so forth or help locate those services to respond to a particular need.

The social committees of the groups keep an active calendar as well. The young singles have a monthly pot luck and talk-it-over with soda and beer for two dollars. Smaller subgroups plan outings to ball games, concerts, and "supper clubs" similar to parish foyer groups, where nine to twelve people gather for dinner.

Often events are planned around holidays, such as a February 14 dinner and movie. "Don't spend your Valentine's Day alone!" the newsletter announces. "No romance allowed!" stresses Treadwell.

His emphasis points up the intentional aspect of the singles' ministry, which is included in the current mission statement. This is not a dating club. It is a place where people can come and be safe; it is fundamentally a community of people who understand and share issues.

Treadwell, like other singles' leaders, points out that he will not give out an individual's telephone number and is not running a dating service. Individuals can become acquainted through the sponsored activities, and if they choose to give out their private telephone numbers, that is their choice.

"Romances do develop," he says. "Slowly. Quietly. There have been a couple of weddings from the group. Basically, we have lots of displays of affection and very little romance."

Both leaders point to the need many singles have to create a sense of family within the larger community of the church. Many are without the support of a family within the geographic area.

The pastoral staff is active in leading retreats and quiet days for singles—men's retreats, women's retreats, coed retreats, age-group retreats. Blackmon prepares a Lenten discipline guide for the singles' community as well. Rogers leads "guilt-free Bible study" groups, planned to enable self-contained study units so that participation is an option.

Currently the single-adult ministry at Saint Michael goes under the umbrella name of Singlepoint: A point where single men and women can gather, learn, serve, and enjoy. A colorful threefold brochure on Singlepoint asks the question "What's the point of Saint Michael's ministry to single people?" The answer? It's a place where singles of many ages and interests can enjoy a Christian community while participating in a wide variety of activities, programs, and service.

The Singlepoint newsletter is published monthly. In keeping with the standard set by the planning committee, it is upbeat, newsy, stimulating—and is mailed to every single person in the parish. That makes the communication personal—an important ingredient for pulling people into the community in a welcoming but nonintrusive way.

Leadership training is also an ongoing component of the program, with Blackmon and Treadwell reaching out to draw in singles' leaders from across the country to help develop the lay leadership in the parish. In this way, the leadership is fresh and energetic, and the program is owned by the community.

Blackmon believes that singles have much to contribute to parish life that often goes unrecognized by the remainder of the congregation. He is quick to point out how he sees this population with whom he has spent over a decade of his ministry; "I think parish churches have much to learn from singles. I have found that singles, in general, have fewer illusions about omnipotence; often they are willing to risk more, and they frequently have come to know themselves better than their married counterparts."

If Blackmon has a continuing concern, it is for the pain of loneliness in American culture, as he continues to see it in his ministry. It is a pain he recognizes as not exclusive to but common among singles.

"There is a lot of loneliness out there," he says. "The church has not begun to take a focused approach to let people know it is aware of their pain. We have to begin to develop ways to walk into a group of single people and help them wrestle with this issue."

Single-Adult Ministry at Village Presbyterian Church in Prairie Village, Kansas

Factor 1. A senior pastor who has detected an area of ministry in need of attention.

Village Presbyterian is a church of 7,800 members begun twenty-two years ago on a postseminary grant to Pastor Bob Meneilly, who has been the parish's only pastor. Ten years ago Meneilly, concerned about the divorced people in his congregation, determined to begin a program for them. He began the search for a director of singles' ministry.

Factor 2. A staff person with special training, ability, and experience in the field.

Meneilly's search led him to Pat Jackard, a midlife-single-again parent. According to Jackard, her special training for the position came in "life and growth." By degree and vocation she was an interior decorator with twenty years of experience as a suburban corporate wife and eight years as a midlife-single-again. Remarried now for five years, she says, "Singleness is woven into the fabric of my being. That is why I am effective at what I do."

Factor 3. A means of financing the program.

Singles' ministry is considered a major priority at Village Presbyterian Church. The congregation commits $100,000 per year to the program and funds Jackard, a project coordinator, and a secretary. The return to the church for this investment is significant. For the past three years, fifty percent of all new member classes have been single.

Factor 4. Determination of priorities in the program.

Pat Jackard and the Singles' Ministry Department are very clear that the order of priority is: (1) God, (2) church, (3) singles' ministry. They believe that a balanced life is the key to wholeness, whether a person is married or single. They believe also that singles' ministry is an outreach ministry to people of all faiths and people of no faith. Jackard calls the ministry "proactive not reactive," based on assessed needs and long-range vision.

Factor 5. A mission statement and flexibility in instituting program.

From the beginning, the philosophy of Village Presbyterian has been to offer "a balanced program of spiritual, educational, psychological, recreational, and social opportunities to singles in the greater Kansas City area. The spiritual component is present in all aspects of the ministry."

The educational aspect of the program was one of the first to be started. There are currently three Sunday school classes for singles. One begins with faith issues as they relate to life. Topics in this class have included Season of Darkness, Season of Light; an Advent class; Faith and Decision Making; Is Your God Too Small? A second class begins with life issues and relates them to faith; topics include Values and Changing Times and Can Humans Forgive? The third class deals with contemporary social or ethical issues, such as God in the Workplace, Ethics, and Sexuality.

A second area of the program combines the educational with the social. On Tuesday evenings a seminar is held throughout the year featuring speakers from the Kansas City area. Topics might vary from psychological issues and relationships to sports and politics, with representatives from the Kansas City Chiefs and Royals appearing one week, members of the ballet company the next.

The Divorce Recovery Seminar is a six-week program held six times each year. Jackard uses "adjunct staff" to lead this high-priority ministry, bringing in local mental health professionals to supplement the ministerial-pastoral staff of the church. She points to the reality of different levels of emotional health within the target population.

"I don't want to indicate that this is a ministry just to the broken. It isn't. Broken is fine, bruised is fine, healthy is fine. We take all. We have all. Presbyterian, Jewish, agnostic."

Jackard points to the ups and downs, accomplishments and things that need more attention in her ministry.

An "up" is the fact that many singles do join the church and move immediately into the life of the whole, while others stay more particularly within the singles' activities.

A sad reality is the fact that the population experiences perhaps one suicide a year.

A real accomplishment is the ministry itself, known throughout the Kansas City area for its integrity.

Jackard is concerned that singles become more mainstreamed into the leadership positions in the church at large.

Factor 6. Ongoing evaluation and adjustment.

Accountability is important to the Village Presbyterian program. This involves regular assessment of the singles' ministry program, being in tune to a population that Jackard describes as "ever changing." What worked last winter may not work this fall.

During the ten years of singles' ministry at Village Presbyterian, it has become known throughout greater Kansas City. The Tuesday evening seminars regularly draw 650 persons. The Divorce Recovery Seminar limits participants to eighty per seminar and maintains a waiting list of fifty. A monthly dance for singles has to be limited to four hundred—admission by ticket only. The ministry maintains a standing contract with the fairgrounds—the only place large enough for the dance. Those in attendance range in age from twenty to sixty.

Many small groups have evolved from the larger activities and represent the interests of the current singles' population. At this writing, those groups include a poets' workshop, an aerobics class, a bridge group, and monthly dinner groups.

A monthly newsletter is considered an essential part of communicating with the target population. It is staffed by some of the 350 volunteers who help keep the ministry going. Jackard sees nurturing and empowering this all-important group as a critical part of her job. Approximately 1,800 single people participate each week in the singles' ministry activities at Village Presbyterian. Some three thousand are on the mailing list.

Jackard does no advertising and says the growth has come about "through word-of-mouth advertising and the integrity of the program." Jackard herself is always actively involved with every aspect of the program, declaring, "I don't want any surprises."

Ministry to Single Adults at Calvary Lutheran Church in Minneapolis

Factor 1. A senior pastor who detected an area of ministry in need of attention.

Calvary is a parish of 7,500 members. The senior pastor of Calvary "gradually" became aware of a growing number of single people in the congregation. His was not an immediate response in terms of staffing, rather a slower collection of data and impressions, a listening to others who were convinced that this was an area that needed special attention. As one who works on a shared-leadership model, his decision was to entrust singles' ministry to a capable person and offer support from the background.

Factor 2. A staff person with special training, experience, and ability in the field.

Laurie Peterson Jeddeloh is associate pastor at Calvary Church. Recently married, she was a single adult when asked to take on this ministry as part of her pastorate. Seminary had offered no specific training in this field. Jeddeloh believes that her own single experience, coupled with "listening to other singles and applying pastoral theology experiences and head knowledge to situations such as forgiveness" were her best training. Knowing that she has been an adult single is an important point of identity for singles in the church.

Factor 3. A plan to finance the ministry.

Once the decision had been made to have a ministry to single adults, the ministry became a part of the church's operating budget. Jeddeloh's salary is not included in her program budget figure of approximately $5,000.

Factor 4. Determination of priorities in the program.

Jeddeloh saw her tasks as:

1. Listening to singles to gauge current needs.
2. Meeting with the best local resources for help—in this case, leaders from local churches of other denominations who have strong singles' ministry programs.
3. Being intentional in applying seminary knowledge concerning marriage and family, chemical dependency and other dependency areas, forgiveness, and so forth to the issues of singles' lives.
4. Educating the church about singles and singles about singles.
5. Promoting singles' leadership in the parish.

Factor 5. A mission statement and flexibility in instituting program.

The mission statement for Calvary Lutheran Singles' Ministry is straight-forward: "Single adults of Calvary are people who are seeking to strengthen themselves and their families through Christian fellowship, praise, prayer, and the proclamation of God's word."

Calvary has three specific groups for singles. The youngest group is postcollege to age forty. (Jeddeloh, like all leaders interviewed, emphasizes that age lines are approximate, not hard and fast.) The goal of this group is to provide a balanced ministry of educational, social, and spiritual opportunities, including bowling, skiing, Bible study, theme retreats, special speakers, and ongoing leadership training.

There is also a group for "forty-something plus" singles. Where the younger group is composed primarily of never-marrieds, the participants in this group are largely single through divorce. While the top age line of the population is "around sixty-five," the majority in this group are forty to fifty-five. They have weekly Bible study and Sunday brunch for fellowship and outreach. They sponsor a Tuesday evening program on issues of singleness; the younger singles are welcome. They are also actively involved with mentoring for the church's confirmation program.

A third group is for single parents, primarily those with children fifteen and under. They meet during the Sunday-school hour for Bible study and support. Once a month they sponsor an event for parents and their children, maybe attending a ball game or going snow tubing. There is little overlap in the three groups.

The church also offers a six-week Divorce Recovery Workshop, which Jeddeloh hopes to see expanded into ongoing groups.

An average of sixty "regular attenders" form the nucleus of this singles' ministry, with "many more people in and out each week." Singles are encouraged to be active in this church or another. Jeddeloh believes that mainstreamed church participation has a good effect on both the singles and the rest of the congregation.

The ministry at Calvary is young, and Laurie Jeddeloh struggles with decisions facing it as it grows: how to keep a Christ-centered ministry; how to be attentive to different needs and emphases?

While some people don't want groups to get "too religious," others are eager for Bible study and more emphasis on the spiritual life. Like other directors of singles' ministries, she deals with a population that includes those who have had "bad" church experiences or no church experience. Despite indication that they want to be there, in a church, there is also hesitancy about spiritual involvement.

Factor 6. Ongoing evaluation and adjustment.

Laurie Peterson Jeddeloh keeps a watchful eye over the singles' ministry at Calvary Lutheran. Because she is acutely aware that (1) she is dealing with a flexible, mobile population and (2) she is in a pioneering ministry, she constantly evaluates her work, making any adjustments as needs become evident.

Jeddeloh has had a growing realization that education and consciousness raising are necessary not only for married persons, but for singles. "We have to deal with the stereotypes that singles have of singles and singleness, that singles have of marrieds, and that marrieds have of singles," she says. To move directly into this issue, the parish has established an annual Singles' Recognition Sunday where singles are ushers, greeters, and musical soloists; they also provide information at special tables before and after worship. Jeddeloh preaches at this service and uses the opportunity to emphasize that the focus of singles' ministry is always to point to the Gospel.

"Sometimes I feel there is a perception that singles' ministry deals only with hurting people, and that's not true," Jeddeloh says. "That is only a portion of the ministry."

She is unaware of any resources or assistance from the national or synod levels of her church. She continues to network with pastors of local nondenominational churches that also have large singles' programs. The Calvary program has become "a place for singles to meet on this side of the city." Its activities are promoted through a regular singles' newsletter, the church newsletter distributed to the full congregation, and for special events, the *Minneapolis Tribune* and on the radio.

Ministry to Single Adults at Holy Innocents Episcopal Church in Atlanta

Factor 1. A senior pastor who has detected an area of ministry in need of attention.

Robert (Bob) Johnson was rector of Holy Innocents Episcopal Church in northern Atlanta before he became bishop of the Diocese of Western North Carolina. During his tenure at Holy Innocents he became aware of the increasing societal trend toward singleness. Then, as rector, and now, as bishop, the subject of ministry to singles is a theological issue for him.

"We are all single," the bishop says. "Some of us just happen to be married. But that doesn't take away my singleness. I am married as long as my marriage lasts . . . that is basic . . . whether it is ended by death or other means of dissolution."

In a Christian education course for the diocese he addressed his theology of singleness, emphasizing that all humans are "singles who happen to be in a unit from time to time."

"If we submerge our individuality," the bishop says, "we forget an important part of who we are. It strengthens marriage to understand this concept."

In getting the singles' ministry off the ground and accepted by his parish, Johnson put all of the pastoral prestige that comes from a long-term tenure at Holy Innocents on the line.

"We sent out the message that this was an intentional ministry. We not only welcomed those who came to us, we as the church would go to where they were with our ministry. We had to be proactive. If that meant going to the local pub, to health clubs, wherever the people were, we went. We had to let them know that the church cared enough to *do* this ministry, cared enough to be criticized for it."

Factor 2. A staff person with special training, experience, and ability in the field.

Enter Dr. John Stathas, a former Roman Catholic priest and psychotherapist, already involved in singles' work. Stathas was introduced to Johnson by a member of the staff.

Stathas believes that his best preparation for this ministry to singles comes from (1) years as a single adult and more recently additional years of being married and (2) counseling skills and training.

He brings to the ministry, he says, a "real strong need to understand the heartbeat, the pulse of any community of which I am a part; a strong sense of where people are in their lives; an ability to lead people to their growth potential; and the fact that I'm not 'preachy'—I like to invite everyone to find their own spirituality—and just emphasize the importance of that quest." Johnson says, "It was crucial that there was a person others saw as the ministry—and could identify with."

Factor 3. A plan to finance the ministry.

From the beginning the ministry, exclusive of Stathas's staff position, has been funded by a three-dollar-per-head fee at Thursday evening seminars and admission fees for special occasions. These monies support a small stipend for the newsletter editor, the production of the newsletter, a small stipend for each program's director, and most activities.

Factor 4. Determination of priorities in the program.

The original priority was established by the rector of the parish when he identified the need to go into those places where singles spent time and minister to them. Other priorities evolved from the beginning.

In addition to responsibilities as program administrator and teacher, Stathas conducts private therapy sessions from a church-provided office. He also keeps a finger on the pulse of the singles' population.

A large percentage of Stathas's therapeutic work is with the singles' population. While some of that work is directly involved with divorce-recovery issues, he also spends considerable time dealing with nonmarital broken relationships, problems of single parenting, and decisions whether to marry or marry again.

The original program of seminars held in popular sports clubs and restaurants has been supplemented by ongoing programs of special-interest groups for tennis playing, concert going, dancing, special study projects, and church and community service. Singles chair and organize the activities and produce and mail the monthly newsletter to approximately two thousand single adults.

Beginning with Bob Johnson's stand on the importance of singles' ministry, the parish of Holy Innocents has been encouraged to include single adults in positions of leadership and policy making.

Factor 5. A mission statement and flexibility in programming.

The mission statement of the Holy Innocents program is specific in defining itself as an outreach ministry to the city of Atlanta; Holy Innocents Church is simply the originator of the ministry. Every Single Person (ESP) has been self-supporting (except for Stathas's salary) since its inception.

Factor 6. Ongoing evaluation and adjustment.

A major time of evaluation came when Bob Johnson was elected bishop and Joe Reynolds was named the new rector of Holy Innocents.

"Joe affirms, values, and supports the program—and gets out of its way so it can work," says Stathas firmly.

When the leadership changed there was no change in emphasis on the involvement of single persons in the leadership of the parish nor in the commitment of the parish to the ministry—a fact that speaks well for Reynolds, Stathas, and the singles' population.

Joe Reynolds knows a working program when he sees one—and ESP works. Recently he presented a seminar on spirituality for the group. His "congregation" contained a spectrum from cradle Episcopalians to agnostics. He and his wife spent the evening dancing with the singles' group at the annual "birthday bash," which celebrates the beginning of the ministry.

He speaks often to his vestry and the parish regarding singles. Says

Stathas, "There is greater intentionality than ever in involving singles in the leadership of the parish."

Today the ESP mailing list contains more than two thousand names —a "very eclectic group," says Stathas. His philosophy is "to connect— not to compete."

Where Two or Three Are Gathered

Many denominations include hundreds of congregations with fewer than three hundred communicants. Such churches may not have the luxury of paid staff beyond the pastor's secretary and perhaps a part-time sexton. A staff person with responsibility for ministry to singles would be un- thinkable. Nor does the smaller church have a broad spectrum of people in any particular grouping of singles. In such churches ministry to single persons takes place more informally but nonetheless intentionally.

The smallest parishes and missions generally maintain a sense of family, struggling together; all who are there—regardless of age or life- style—are "in it together." As parishes grow, they move beyond that stage of involvement and reach what developmentally could be called "the awkward age": too large for everyone to know one another and be involved in everything; too small for multistaff, multidivision, maxi- population kinds of opportunities.

It is simply no longer acceptable to say, "We're too small to have singles' ministry," or, "We don't have any singles here."

Singles' ministry is, first of all, an attitude.

The church that says it does not minister to singles because it has no singles will not only be a small church, it will soon be a dying church. The truth is in the numbers. If forty-eight percent of the population of adults in the United States is single and there are no single adults in a congregation, there is something amiss!

Ministry to singles in the smaller church has at least five components:

Component 1. The senior minister will have informed awareness of the issues and an ongoing intention of including singles in all aspects of parish life.

Mike Lumpkin, rector of Saint Christopher's, a small church in

Spartenburg, South Carolina, was single until his early thirties. The
memory of feeling as if he lived in "a very coupled world" has influenced Lumpkin's concept of ministry—and the intentional nature of his
ministry to singles. His informed awareness grows out of personal experience that he can now translate into his leadership of the parish.

For those clergy who have never lived as single adults—how to
become informed and aware?

While resources within the denominations studied—Episcopal,
Presbyterian Church USA, and Evangelical Lutheran—have to date been
limited, efforts are being made to produce educational materials, both
printed and audiovisual, that will assist local churches and regional bodies in obtaining information on this topic. Moving across other denominational lines, I've listed a number of helpful resources in the bibliography.

Each pastor, associate, or assistant would do well to read in four
specific areas (see bibliography):

1. Theology and philosophy of family of God, and how that mani-
   fests itself in programming. (Resource: Janet Fishburn, *Confronting the Idolatry of Family: A New Vision for the Household
   of God.*)
2. Demographics concerning the lives of single people in America.
   (Resource: Carolyn Koons and M. J. Anthony, *Single Adult
   Passages: Uncharted Territory.*)
3. The scope of ministry to single people. (Resources: John D.
   Vogelsang, *Singleness and Community: Toward the Whole
   People of God* [manuscript]; Douglas Fagerstrom, ed., *Singles'
   Ministry Handbook;* Jerry Jones, ed., *Single Adult Ministry.*)
4. Singles' spirituality. (Resource: Susan Muto, *Celebrating the
   Single Life: A Spirituality for Single Persons in Today's World.*)

**Component 2. The minister will intentionally prepare parish leader-
ship and membership for one-on-one ministry to singles by educating them in the issue and including single adults in key leadership
positions.**

Mike Lumpkin remembers that, as a single lay person, life could be
lonely. He often filled his calendar to overflowing as a way of avoiding
the loneliness. Some singles become workaholics for the same reason.

Says Lumpkin, "Whatever the particulars, singles don't always volunteer for things. They need to be asked, and asked again." Lumpkin is also intentional in sending personal letters to singles when there is an upcoming event, not just leaving it to the bulletin or a general mailing to entice them to come. Nominating committees are instructed to include singles in their nominations, as are those forming committees.

Bishop Bob Johnson, speaking to his days in the parish, says, "It is important to always have a single person on the vestry . . . for the nominating committee always to nominate with that in mind. There should be singles on all major parish committees, in major leadership roles. The word gets out. This is not just a church for married people; this is also a church that welcomes and includes singles at every level of its life."

To help parish leadership fully understand the concept of singles' ministry and the underlying theology, the senior minister can circulate copies of resources to the parish leadership and congregation and invite speakers on the subject to address classes and special meetings.

Component 3: The parish will encourage small groups around singles' issues, being flexible as to inter- or intra-church configurations at a given time, and develop lay leadership among singles.

It is important that churches have an opportunity to re-identify themselves through small group discussions that help individuals get rid of stereotypes of individuals and groups and dig for the genesis of the current paradigm.

Holly Salisbury, of Saint Peter's Episcopal Church in Paris, Kentucky, says that one of the most helpful educational pieces for her came from the opening session of a recent singles' conference when the Rev. Canon Louis "Skip" Schueddig of Atlanta spoke of combing the New Testament for Jesus' words concerning family; he found only fourteen references—none of which referred to the nuclear family and all of which were radical in nature, such as "leave your father and your mother."

Janet Fishburn's book on the idolatry of family is particularly helpful in stimulating conversation concerning where this idea of family began and how it has been translated into the lives of our churches. With a presentation on Fishburn's ideas used as a starting point, congregations can then move into dialogue on the realities of family in modern life.

Again, small group or Sunday school formats are excellent for looking at stereotypes—of singles about singles, of singles about marrieds, of marrieds about singles. As one minister of a small parish said, "I've never been an adult single person. I don't have any idea what that life is like. So I assume it is like mine." Structured conversation in this area can assist in such dialogue. [See Appendix 1 for group designs.]

Component 4. The parish will share ministry with neighboring/like churches, across denominational lines.

Shared ministry within denominations and across denominational lines is essential to smaller churches.

Churches in close proximity within a synod, diocese, or presbytery might join together for regular programs or special-interest groups. Churches of different denominations within a given neighborhood, area, or city could join forces on the same basis. In Lexington, Kentucky, St. Michael's Episcopal and Faith Lutheran Churches in the southeastern area of the city have recently joined forces to offer monthly social and program activities from theater parties to discussions on Lutheran-Episcopal dialogue.

Component 5. The parish will assist and encourage interested singles to be involved with singles' work on a regional and national level. This work would provide personal growth and further educate the parish in terms of understanding the new demographics and what they mean to parish life. From such an education, parish dialogue and plans can develop.

While participation in regional and nationwide activities is generally helpful to anyone, it is a particularly important way for the person in the small parish to feel connected to a larger group and to gain access to important information and education for the parish itself.

The pastor of the small church should note brochures and letters on this subject that cross the desk, passing them along to singles who might be interested. The pastor can also encourage the parish leadership to allocate funds from the general budget or a special projects fund to assist participation.

Chapter Summary

Let's summarize the findings of this chapter in terms of the six factors discussed as being critical to a thriving single-adult ministry.

Factor 1. A pastor who recognizes singles' ministry as an area in need of attention is key in developing this ministry, regardless of the size of the congregation. In a large congregation the appropriate action resulting from this awareness will include the development of theology, attitude, staff, and program. For the smaller parish this awareness will be evident in the development of theology and attitude.

Factor 2. A staff person with special training, experience, and ability in the field has been significant in each larger parish ministry. While the backgrounds of the individuals vary, each has had experience as an adult single person in addition to other education, credentials, and personal attributes. In a smaller parish a volunteer who can work as adjunct to the paid staff or pastor could raise the awareness of the congregation and serve as a liaison with other singles' programs.

Factor 3. For the ministry to become firmly established, a church must have a plan to finance the ministry at whatever budgetary level is feasible. Three out of four parishes studied made singles' ministry a line item in the operating budget of the parish. The fourth ministry, an outreach ministry in a large urban center, is self supporting.

Factor 4. Determination of priorities in the program involves:

1. Priorities in approach to the program (from the perspective of the leader). These include:
   a. Research successful programs to learn about other singles' ministries.
   b. Network with singles' leaders at a local base as well as at each level of denomination and other denominations.
   c. Become part of interdenominational singles' leadership organizations and other training opportunities.
   d. Educate staff, parish leadership, congregation, and singles themselves.

2. Priorities within the program itself:
   a. Determine the age and interest groups with greatest needs as a starting place.

    b. Develop mission statement and build from that statement.
    c. Involve core group in planning process.
    d. Provide leadership training for lay leaders.
    e. Evaluate and adjust on an ongoing basis.

Factor 5. Early in the ministry the church developed a mission statement for the singles' ministry and instituted a program with flexibility.

While each program studied had its own unique beginning and list of priorities, there were similar components in the early stages. The development of a mission statement helped keep the ministry focused. The determination to keep programs balanced in spiritual, educational, psychological, social, and recreational aspects contributed to the ability to attract a diverse population and age groups. Remaining flexible and continually assessing the program have helped the target population feel that their interests and needs have been taken seriously.

Factor 6. Because of the changing nature of the population, ongoing evaluation and adjustment in the program are perhaps more essential in singles' ministry than other specialized ministries. Leaders exhibit a willingness to understand this flexibility factor and use it as an integral component of the ministry.

The programs that have been built, the attitudes that have been birthed at Saint Michael and All Angels, at Calvary, at Village Presbyterian, at Holy Innocents, and at Saint Christopher's are examples of a new core ministry in the church.

They built.

The singles come.

CHAPTER III

Doing the Church, Being the Church

What Does 'Help from the Church' Mean?

When single church members talk of developing ministry to single adults, they often ask for "help from the church."

The church, as it is used here, seems to carry a threefold meaning: (1) the specific local congregation, (2) the denomination, and (3) the church at large. Recognition from each of these levels lifts any issue from a pioneer stage, marked by a minority crying for serious attention, to a "given" position in the institution. At this stage the question is no longer "Will there be ministry to single people in the church?" but "What specific role will each level of the institution play in the ministry?"

There are life areas on which church members know their denominations take official positions: marriage, divorce, sexuality. Theologies are developed around these issues. When an issue reaches this level of concern, it becomes a part of the philosophical, theological, and educational fabric of the denomination, to be considered in preparation for ministry—in funding, in prioritizing, planning, and program.

Single adults have been excluded from this level of the church-at-large primarily because the church, as an institution, has long seen itself in terms of the nuclear family. Attention is beginning to be focused on ministry to single adults by some denominational leaders, mandated primarily by the sheer force of numbers and requests for assistance from local and regional groups.

The sample denominations in this study—the Episcopal, Presbyterian Church USA, and Evangelical Lutheran Church in America (ELCA)—consider the base or grassroots level of their denominations the diocese, presbytery, or conference. These units are made up of local congregations in a geographical area. The diocese belongs to a larger province, the presbytery to a synod, the conference to a synod.

The churches in these local units have an interdependence that is part and parcel of who the church is as experienced in each of the three denominations. These levels of the church are not simply exercises in hierarchy and authority; they represent in essence a unity and interdependence in churches that recognize both their separateness and their identity as one body of Christ. Therefore, when a voice from the pew expresses the need or desire to have a response "from the church," that voice expresses more than the desire to have a title attached to a desk at a national office. Concerned congregants expect linkage and interdependence concerning theology, philosophy, and priority.

Considering this expectation, it is important to look to the structures of these three denominations to identify examples of existing positions and philosophies in the regional and national levels of the church and to see how the church structures might be more effectively tapped for this ministry. After all, the diocese, the presbytery, the synod, the province, the conference, indeed, the national churches, are not a "they" but a "we."

Frustration in the Field, Denominational Response

First: an assessment of why, in the grass roots, it feels as though there is neither attention nor intention toward singles' issues in terms of resources, referrals, and communication.

Begin by mentally placing yourself at a telephone somewhere in Indiana, South Dakota, Pennsylvania, Arizona, Ohio, Wyoming, or Kentucky. The purpose of the telephone call about to be made is to gather information to assist in a project for singles within a diocese, synod, or presbytery that, at this time, has no resources.

According to laity, calls placed to Presbyterian and Episcopal national and regional headquarters asking for "the person in charge of singles' ministry" result in the response "no one is listed with that title." Conversations with numerous offices follow before the caller might end up with the friendly and helpful voices of staff persons currently in charge of the "single portfolio." A call to the ELCA headquarters rings through to the Family and Single Office of the Division for Congregational Ministries.

According to Sherry Harbaugh of the ECLA, policy from the national or church-wide offices of these three denominations is "responsive to local issue-based organizations rather than mandates from the top."

In the hinterlands, restless singles feel that there is an issue and no responsiveness—on any level.

Harbaugh of the ELCA reports "no top-down authority on ministry to singles in the ELCA, but an encouragement to synod assemblies for educational events around the entire issue of singleness. The philosophy of the church-wide office is inclusiveness, for singles to be in solidarity with the whole." The Family and Single Office is currently involved in publishing a resource for university- or seminary-level information on this issue in a cooperative project with the Episcopal Church.

In the Minneapolis Synod where Janet Grant is a part-time staff person for singles' ministry, the idea of inclusivity and solidarity is philosophically sound, but practically unrealistic. "In order to educate, empower, and enable, it is necessary to have singles' groups and to do lots of education of the whole church," says Grant. "I open every talk I make with the statement that I really don't believe in singles' ministry at all but that I don't believe we'll not need it in my lifetime."

There is "awareness of singles' issues from many different perspectives" at 815 Second Avenue in New York City, the headquarters of the Episcopal Church. The Office of Evangelism supported a locally generated resolution to the 1991 General Convention of the Church to be more intentional toward singles and to evaluate where the Church is on this issue. The Offices of Family and Christian Education are "involving single people in conversation" in their planning process.

A few years back, in an attempt toward both a national leaders' network and provincial events, a 1988 conference for leaders and other singles was followed by a broader-based event known as Families 2000. With the internal restructuring necessitated by budget cuts, there is now "nothing pending," with the exception of the publishing project with ELCA and efforts to establish provincial communications and resource and communications data bases.

The Rev. Linda Grenz of the Episcopal Church Center staff cites the need for video and printed resources and training of trainers to develop leadership in the provinces.

At the diocesan level, only two or three dioceses have a listing for a person in charge of or responsible for the concept of singles' ministry.

The Diocese of Lexington has developed a model for conjoint ministry of the diocese and cathedral and is seeking a grant to fund its further development.

"Singles" has been added to the title of the Family Office at the Presbyterian Church USA national headquarters in Louisville, Kentucky. Although the General Assembly of the Church has called for attention to single-adult issues, "part of the reality" is that the discussions are just beginning. Ray Trout, executive for family and singles, looks toward denomination-wide consultations that will help develop resources and leadership for the area.

"It is not a matter of writing and talking theology," Trout says, "as much as looking at the issue of how an institution so family oriented can, in effect, change its lifestyle. It is a fundamental issue: the diversity of the family configuration. We are hampered by a model of 'doing' church based on a particular and partial concept of being the church family . . .

"This has been a major barrier. It is a major challenge to be inclusive. We need greater clarity on the issue at all levels of the Church—and greater dollars—even as we face the reality of the economic situation."

Regardless of denomination, the frustration in the field is real. Says Lutheran pastor Dorothy Feithtner of Terre Haute, Indiana, "I've given up working through the church, and that's a shame because that's where it needs to be. I've just run out of energy." Feithtner, minister to a congregation of some 220, looks at the stacks of work on her desk. "I pushed to get something done at the synod level. There were no resources, no help. The response was 'You want something done? You do it!' Frankly, I've run out of steam trying to convince them of the importance of being the church in this ministry, so I'm doing the ministry though the 'Y.' "

At present many efforts at singles' ministry have been short-lived, not from lack of need but from lack of institutional interest as well as support. Many Dorothys have "run out of energy." The efforts that do exist are clearly grassroots, often with leadership frustrated by lack of a network and intent on staying within church boundaries to give singles' work a spiritual base. National organizations—overwhelmed by lack of funds and too many and diverse demands on existing staff—could offer channels for communication and referral of specialists to harness the expertise and energy that is already in the field.

Important Issues Exist in Singles' Ministry

This is not the time for hierarchal flow charts that cover the issue on paper but do not connect with leaders in the grassroots areas or make it past restructuring and staff changes. This is *not* a small issue, to be confused with parlor games, dating, and mating. This business of ministry to single adults cuts across the heart of ministry in the church at large, mandating theological position and attention to issues of major societal, developmental, and spiritual import—issues that until now have been possible to consider "unusual" or "out of the mainstream."

These issues include (1) an understanding of singleness as the essential state in which we are born, come to God, and die; (2) the evangelizing of minority populations with the realization that singles numerically will soon be the majority of the population; (3) Christian education—as it touches the real issues in the lives of people today and relates those issues to the Gospel; (4) sexuality and singleness—what are the patterns, root problems, and their causes? What is the theology of sexuality?; (5) spiritual hunger— is the church taking the opportunity for spiritual development into the heart of darkness of those who are alone and uniquely ripe for a relationship with the One who truly answers that aloneness?

In large denominations, such as the Episcopal, Presbyterian, and ELCA, these issues cannot be dealt with only from a local-issue, congregational base. Projects may well be generated from such a base, but the prioritizing, the policy making, the emphasis and direction flow from the top. It's time to move beyond the piecemeal and putting-out-fires approach to the issue. The existing structures contain within themselves the beginning of the network that can connect, educate, and empower. Its links must be strengthened; its conduits opened for the energy to flow.

Broad Leadership Must Respond—Integrate

In the *Singles' Ministry Handbook,* edited by Douglas Fagerstrom, Jim Smoke, a pioneer in the area of singles' ministry and author of several books on the subject, says that all singles' ministry should include: (1) recovery room ministry, (2) maintenance ministry, and (3) leadership in the church by singles.[1]

I would like to add to that list *integrated ministry,* focusing local and denominational church leadership on the fact that the work they do or do not do in terms of ministry to single adults is directly connected to the vital areas of youth and young adults, family life, evangelism, and spirituality.

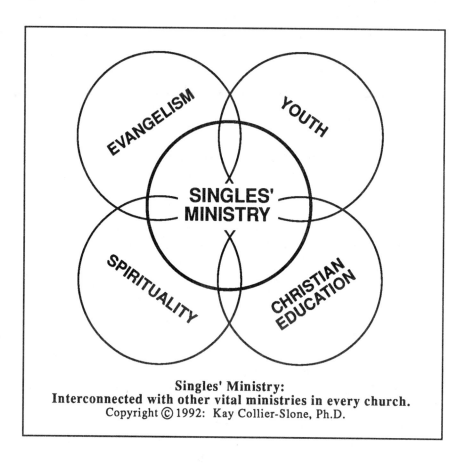

Singles' Ministry:
Interconnected with other vital ministries in every church.
Copyright © 1992: Kay Collier-Slone, Ph.D.

How singles' ministry "looks" and is programmed must remain flexible if it is to be responsive to local situations. While Smoke writes about models for ministry involving large, multistaff parishes with congregational government, his criteria fit equally well with a diocesan, conference, or presbytery structure serving both large and small congregations.

National offices in all three denominations appear to be struggling with time, money and energy for this complex issue. In light of the economic issues in all three denominations, the reality of the "broad sensitivity to the needs of single people" and "growing recognition of singles and their special concerns" does not seem to be felt at the grass-roots level; these matters must be brought to the immediate attention of broad leadership. Standing commissions and other interim bodies govern denominations between national meetings. These bodies are composed of clergy and laity from local congregations across the country. As these persons—who sit on committees concerning family, evangelism, parish growth, program, budget and finance, and spiritual formation—consider the issues and dollars before them, it would be well for them to consider the following:

Youth and Christian education, working in conjunction with singles' ministry, must evaluate curriculum with regard to focus on solitude/ personal wholeness/self-esteem moving toward "seasons of singleness" as normal parts of the life cycle. Both the married state and the single state must be viewed as normal life choices for healthy, whole human beings.

Curriculum at all levels must be based on a theology of humanity that embraces the realities of life while reaching for the ideal.

Evangelism must be in touch with singles' leaders and programs to learn how to reach singles in the community who do not have a church home. "Recovery-room ministry" must come to be viewed as a facet of evangelism, as well as a facet of the healing ministry. As one woman, still in the recovery stages following divorce, said of her choice of the Episcopal Church, "I wasn't sure that the ritual would ever be comfortable for this ex-Baptist. But I had been coming to divorce-recovery group for over a year, and the parking lot and the door to the building were familiar—not one other new thing to be conquered." Evangelism in one of its more subtle forms—but evangelism still!

Those who are concerned with spiritual formation and development must work with singles' leaders in providing training and leadership to speak to the very real need singles have to understand their lives in relation to a Gospel that often seems interpreted "for nuclear families only."

New liturgical options must be provided.

Liturgical Offerings Make Statements

The single state of being has not had rituals and symbols that affirm and bless it. It is time to affirm singles, to bless them, and to offer experiences in the church that allow single individuals to view themselves and their lives as open to the mystery and the transcending power of God.

In his book *Living in Sin?* (published by HarperCollins Publishers), Bishop John Spong, Bishop of Newark, New Jersey, asks the question,

> What would it mean to have the church offer a liturgical service to mark the end of a marriage? Would it serve, as some suggest, only to encourage people to seek divorces? Would it bring a note of grace and redemption to one of life's moments of brokenness? Would it enable people who were not able to keep the marriage vows to experience more forgiveness than guilt? Does the church really want to lessen guilt, or is it the conscious and unconscious fear of all ecclesiastical structure that if guilt is lessened so also will be motivation and control? What would such a service look like, feel like, and accomplish?[2]

Such are the questions that have arisen time and time again among singles and with clergy who are willing to talk about the issue.

Bishop Spong includes in his book "a service for the recognition of the end of a marriage." He says,

> Both the men and the women were and are committed Christians, and the church that had been a central focus of their marriage somehow also had to be the focus of their separation. Hence, this service—painful, traumatic, but intensely real—was planned to offer this all-new, too-human reality called divorce to God, and to seek healing and new directions from this God for these lives.

In Spong's service the Prayers of the People include these words:

> On behalf of the church which blessed your marriage, we now recognize the end of that marriage. We affirm you as single persons among us, and we pledge you our support as you continue to seek God's help and guidance for the new life you have undertaken in faith.[3]

Bishop Spong lists six important impressions for the use of this service:

1. First, pain and death are present in divorce for both the husband and the wife, whether recognized liturgically or not.
2. It takes courage, maturity, and a willingness to endure enormous vulnerability to stand up, even among invited close friends, confess failure, and ask forgiveness.
3. Sometimes the fraction and bitterness of divorce are so bitter that one or both of the partners could not or would not choose to avail such an experience.
4. A funeral service for someone you love is also painful and difficult, but a pain and a difficulty that enables growth.
5. Every common experience is a bonding experience in which lives and relationships are redefined. This service enables this man and this woman to begin the process of relating to each other in a new way.
6. Without compromising the essential commitment to the ideal of faithful, monogamous marriage, the church needs to proclaim that divorce is sometimes the alternative that gives hope for life, and that marriage is sometimes the alternative that delivers only death.[4]

Where sufficient communication exists for a couple, liturgies of divorce can be helpful, not only to the immediate family, but to extended family and friends who are also "victims" in these situations. Clergy and counselors report increased need for pastoral assistance from family and friends of any couple going through divorce. Likewise, the need exists to close one way of relating (marriage) and begin a new way (postmarriage). A recognition and solemnization of that closure and new beginning might offer real hope for mediating healthy communication in the years ahead.

One divorced woman told of her search for an Episcopal priest who would assist her in having a service of closure and blessing of her new life when her ex-spouse chose not to participate. Her desire to solemnize this occasion in the church proper was rejected by her bishop who did not want to "bless divorce." But she was to find help from another priest who, under the guidance of Rite Three ("An Order for Celebrating the Eucharist") in *The Book of Common Prayer,* assisted in the design and celebration of a divorce liturgy and blessing of singleness. The service was adapted from *Liturgy in Learning through the Life Cycle* by John Westerhoff and William H. Willimon.[5] [See Appendix 5.]

At Christ Church Cathedral in Lexington, Kentucky, the idea for a liturgy of healing and wholeness recognizing the end of marriage and blessing of singleness grew out of the divorce-recovery ministry. The bishop understood the need and authorized the dean of the cathedral to work with the coordinator of singles' ministry to develop a service that would be within the boundaries of the canon law of the church and diocese. The service takes place on the Wednesday of Holy Week to symbolize the death-and-resurrection nature of the divorce-recovery process. Those who have worked in the divorce-recovery groups are invited to participate in the service if they feel ready to do so, and they may invite family and close friends to share in the service. Those currently in the process of divorce recovery are also encouraged to participate as the supporting community and offer the hope of wholeness and healing that they also will achieve. This service allows participants to experience Holy Week in a deeper way and move into their own personal Easter experiences as single individuals—whole and healed. Based on the service for the Sacrament of Healing, the service is called "The Liturgy of Healing and Wholeness." [See Appendix 5.]

Such liturgies offer the opportunity for a semipublic, corporate acknowledgment and acceptance of the new status. They help eradicate the sense of shame and failure and raise the individual and the status to a new level of normalcy. These services also provide opportunity for struggling newly single people to involve their new support systems in their lives sacramentally and to own their own resurrection and transformation.

It is important that clergy be open to using such liturgies in the church proper, as divorced singles in particular have a real need to be assured that they are "okay" in the eyes of the church.

Still another liturgical option involves opportunities for those who experience grief, even ongoing grief (and this option certainly extends far beyond the singles' community), to acknowledge their grief and loss in some specific ritual, particularly around holiday services such as Christmas and Easter. Ritualizing is very critical to the grief process, whether the loss be through death or divorce. Often official services of worship are painful reminders of what once was formerly shared and is no longer.

At Christ Church Episcopal Cathedral a series of classes—Grief and the Holidays—acknowledges this pain and offers an optional worship experience at the final service. The service, which grows out of the needs of the participants, generally includes lighting of candles signifying the giving into God's keeping that which has or those who have been lost. The Eucharist is celebrated in an act of transformation and redemption. [See Appendix 5.]

Regularizing such liturgical options would allow clergy to offer the healing power of these services to those who might not be aware of their availability or acknowledge their own personal need, but who would benefit greatly from the services.

A Model for Cojoint Ministry

From my observation the most comprehensive work being done in singles' ministry today is in large, multistaff, congregational churches. Churches, such as the Episcopal, Presbyterian, and Lutheran, that work under a diocesan, presbytery, or conference structure have a major strength for ministry—if the structure is used effectively.

When the base unit—diocese, presbytery, or conference that has an established sense of interconnectedness and works under a common central authority—is used as an organizing unit, congregations of all sizes have an opportunity to become involved in a ministry for which local funding and staffing might not be available. The base unit also provides an area larger than a parish from which to draw participants with similar needs and interests.

One such model has been developed in the Episcopal Diocese of Lexington, Kentucky, as a conjoint effort between the diocese and the cathedral; the two share a staff member in the position of coordinator of ministries to single adults.

This model will be considered using the six factors from chapter 2.

Factor 1. A senior pastor who detected an area of ministry in need of attention.

In this instance, recognition of the need for ministry came from the laity who, under a volunteer chairperson, established the Task Force on

Ministry to Single Adults and presented a resolution to the diocesan convention to establish a Commission on Singles' Ministry. The bishop and the dean of the cathedral, when presented with the data, embraced the concept and appointed a coordinator of singles' ministry.

Factor 2. A staff person with special training, experience, and ability in the field.

The coordinator of this ministry is a single lay woman who holds a Ph.D. in counseling psychology with subspecialties in grief recovery, divorce recovery, group dynamics, life transitions, and singleness. Her existing position on the diocesan staff enabled her to begin work in a part-time capacity from an already established office.

Factor 3. A plan to finance the ministry.

In the early stages of the work, programs went forward with assistance from the bishop's discretionary fund, the dean's discretionary fund, surplus monies from other commissions in the Department of Ministry of the Diocese, to which the Commission was assigned. The long-range plan calls for grant monies to be supplemented by cathedral and diocesan monies on a five-year plan until the program is fully funded by joint budgetary efforts of diocese and cathedral at a beginning level of $30,000.

Factor 4. Determination of priorities in the program.

The first business of the Task Force on Singles' Ministries was to begin to identify who the single people in the diocese were and what their needs were. This information, together with data gathered by the coordinator in meeting and talking with singles, would assist in prioritizing.

The original list of priorities, as developed in this manner, was as follows:

1. Divorce recovery ministry
2. Social and networking ministry for midlife singles

3. An ongoing diocesan commission
4. Special-needs events
   a. For the cathedral
   b. For the diocese
   c. Ecumenically
5. Formational educational programs
   a. Sunday-school class for singles
   b. Spiritual-educational Sunday-afternoon programs
6. Communication and promotion
7. Spiritual development
8. Young-singles' ministry
9. Older singles' programs
10. Outreach
11. Leadership training.

Factor 5. A mission statement and flexibility around instituting program.

The ministry established, called Intergenerational Ministries to Single Adults, acknowledges its need for and commitment to:

1. God
2. Church
3. Each other
4. Singles' ministry program

With these recognitions in mind, Intergenerational Ministries (for, of, and by single adults) is a place where single adults from postcollege through postretirement can be in a safe and caring community of people who understand and share issues; where they are involved in life-long spiritual, intellectual, emotional, and physical growth and wish to promote effective interaction, communication, leadership and service within the parish, diocese, and community. Single adults of all faiths are welcome.

In 1989 the Divorce Recovery Ministry began as an independent, professionally led support group that used cathedral facilities on an ongoing basis.

Two other aspects of the ministry began simultaneously in the fall of

1990. It was apparent that midlife singles at the cathedral needed a social-networking outlet. A small group of midlife singles began meeting once a month for a pot luck or some other planned outing and one Wednesday night a month at a local restaurant for dinner after the healing service. At the same time the Task Force formed on a diocesan basis and set about identifying singles, writing a resolution for diocesan convention, and planning a diocesan-wide event.

During Advent 1990, the first Grief and the Holidays seminar was held. This three-session program is designed to help through the holidays any person suffering from any loss. Sessions carry the following titles:

Session 1: It's the Holidays and I Don't Feel Like Celebrating
Session 2: Others Have Walked This Path Before
Session 3: In Sacrament and Symbol We Remember

In spring 1991 the Commission sponsored a diocesan-wide event, Love and Lent, for which singles from across the diocese came to the cathedral the first Saturday of Lent for a pot luck brunch and Lenten quiet day. The cathedral also sponsored three six-week classes called K.I.D.S. (Kids in Divorce Situations) for elementary, middle-school, and high-school/college-age young people who have gone or are going through a divorce experience in their family.

Factor 6. Ongoing evaluation and adjustment.

In the late summer and early fall of 1991, the coordinator began a series of evaluation sessions with persons who had been participating in or leading various singles' events. Those evaluation sessions were followed up with consultations with the dean and the singles' commission.

The following program additions were planned:

Singles' Sunday- chool class,
    also Singularly Significant Brunch Bunch
Overnight retreat
Young singles' program
Senior singles' brainstorming
Additional support activities
Monthly newsletter including calendar

The Singularly Significant Sunday school class is a Bible study based on the Serendipity series that promotes discussion.[6] Seasonal classes—a Lenten series—covered topics such as Angels, Discipleship, and Discernment. The Singularly Significant Brunch Bunch meets at a local restaurant on the second Sunday of each month.

The first overnight retreat for singles was held at the diocesan conference center. The title of the planned retreat series is Discovery, to indicate the desire of the group to continue their learning. The theme of the first conference was Loneliness, Intimacy, and Sexuality. The Rev. Canon Louis Schueddig of Atlanta led the retreat. Bishop Wimberly named that Sunday "Singles' Sunday" in the diocese. Retreatants and Schueddig returned to Lexington, where Schueddig preached two services at the cathedral and led the dean's Sunday-school class, providing a major educational session for the congregation.

A relationship dependency group was added to the list of support activities available at the cathedral. Within the diocese, three parishes have notified the commission that they are beginning organized ministry to singles within their parishes. Commission members continue to seek names of contact persons from each parish and mission as the basis for communication within the diocese.

In late winter and early spring of 1992, the cathedral planned its first interdenominational activity with First Presbyterian Church, its neighbor across the street. The Presbyterians hosted a four-week class for both churches—Flying Solo: The Loneliness Factor. The cathedral sponsored a Valentine's activity for both churches. The event, A Heartful Afternoon, included an old-fashioned Valentine's tea, followed by a recital and choral evensong.

The coordinator's meetings with young singles and senior singles resulted in information that would be translated into action: (1) Young singles want Bible study and a name that does not use the term *single*. (2) Senior singles want occasional planned activities in addition to what is already offered and help for inclusion in already existing activities (rides to evening activities, etc.). (3) Sunday afternoon and evening are the times of greatest loneliness for all age groups.

TNT Saints and Sinners kicked off its Bible study for twenty-something and thirty-something singles. A single female seminarian was recruited to lead this group, to comply with the young singles' request that the leader be knowledgeable, relatively near their ages, and have some understanding of the single lifestyle.

To attend to the issue of Sunday afternoon loneliness, the cathedral plans a once-a-month series, Dimensions: Sunday Singles' Series, which will explore various issues, such as, Respite Care Facilities for the Mentally Ill; Seasons of Singleness: Opportunities for Deepening Spirituality; Female and Priest: Experience and Contribution; Transition: Making the Most of Life's Changes; and Dependencies: Moving On without Crutches.

The diocesan commission sponsored Discovery II, a two-night retreat at the conference center and formed a long-range planning committee. Commission members make themselves available to give educational talks about singleness to vestries and other groups.

A monthly newsletter and calendar is produced by staff.

A special Liturgy of Healing and Wholeness, for the acknowledgment of the end of a marriage and blessing of singleness, is held on the Wednesday of Holy Week.

In the immediate future, plans include: (1) formation of a singles' cathedral council for evaluation and planning; (2) development of a resource center for singles in conjunction with the Cathedral and Diocesan Resource Center and Library; (3) regional singles' events in the diocese with the commission going "on the road" to cohost the events and offer regional teacher training, leadership-parish awareness; and (4) participation in regional and national singles' activities. This model for ministry is replicable in any regional-denominational structure with a minimum of one staff person trained in ministry to singles. The terms *cathedral/diocese* could be interchanged with *presbytery/synod* or *conference/synod,* or the central organizing body could be a cardinal or corporate-sized parish working with other churches in a geographic region.

In dioceses, synods, or presbyteries where the area is great and the communicant strength sufficient, the staff person could have several districts under his or her jurisdiction.

In summary, this model:

1. Begins from the structure of the denomination, the diocese, presbytery, or conference working with a cathedral or cardinal parish and a trained staff person.
2. Identifies (a) singles and (b) areas of need.
3. Institutionalizes the ministry for purposes of education, program, and funding.

From this base, activities are added and new priorities drawn.

Seminaries Must Offer Singles' Ministry Training

At a denomination's top levels attention should be drawn to seminary training and continuing education of clergy. At present none of the major seminaries in the three denominations studied is known to include in its pastoral theology or field education extensive training concerning singleness.

The Rev. Dr. Will Spong, director of pastoral care at the (Episcopal) Seminary of the Southwest in Austin, Texas, includes singleness issues in what he calls his "Pastoral Medley"—"four or five of the 'hot' topics facing the church. Issues like singleness, racism, AIDS." He sees the issue as moving clergy away from "marital absorption—helping them understand that singleness is not a matter of better or worse, only different, whether they came to singleness by necessity or decision."

Janet Grant of the Minneapolis Synod (ELCA) points to a difficulty in keeping anyone from the Lutheran seminaries on her synod singles' board. "It's not an issue being attended to in the seminaries," she states. At Lutheran Northwestern (ELCA), the largest Lutheran seminary in the United States, she points to "seven shelves of books on marriage and three-quarters of a shelf, about thirty titles, on singleness. Most of those were written in the eighties." The Rev. Dr. Phillip Culbertson, former professor of pastoral theology at Saint Luke's School of Theology (Episcopal) in Sewanee, Tennessee, says, "It is not dealt with in the curriculum to any great degree. I try to include a couple of hours of lecture from a multigenerational view, including the elderly, many of whom are single."

Culbertson feels that singleness is not dealt with in "a lump—in one place at this time, but rather weaving through the entire picture of human life."

At Louisville Presbyterian Seminary, Professor of Pastoral Theology Nancy Ramsey says that at present there are no courses on the issue itself, but she sees new and emerging courses beginning to address singleness.

A new course, Family Systems in Culture and Context, will look at singleness as a fact, an increasing way of being, not an interim period in life. In a course titled Sex and Pastoral Practice, students will look at ethics of sexuality, with norms and guidelines for expressing sexuality. Hermeneutical issues will also be considered: the sexuality reports of the church, assumptions about sexuality, norms of sexuality. A class on aging also addresses singleness within the aging population.

If the church is to minister effectively to its people in the twenty-first century, it is mandatory that the clergy be informed of and educated in issues of singleness and prepared to develop appropriate attitudes as well as programs in their parishes—regardless of the parish size.

Today the church, at all levels of the structures, is struggling to catch up with a paradigm that has already begun. Members and prospective members of the church are living in that paradigm and asking for attention and intention that they might be the church as they go about the business of doing the church.

CHAPTER IV

What Does Singles' Ministry Look Like?

Some basic ingredients appear to be important to the establishment and maintenance of a ministry to single adults. These principles appear again and again, in writing, in conversations with pastors and singles' leaders, with singles themselves.

1. A theology of humanity that embraces singleness as a normal, optional state of beingness.
2. The support of the senior pastor and church leadership.
3. Strong professional leadership by a person with both training and experience in the single adult world.
4. A mission statement representative of a balanced ministry.
5. An opportunity for telling stories and listening.
6. Flexibility in dealing with a "flexible" population.
7. Sensitivity in naming of program and activities.
8. Understanding the needs of the target population.
9. Singles' Sunday school class—an entry point and more.
10. Networking—putting people in touch with other people.
11. Balanced ministry—spiritual, emotional, intellectual, physical, and social.
12. Publicity: frequent, well done, upbeat, and personal.
13. A council of single people to assist in planning.
14. Lay leadership and a core group of involved individuals who take ownership of the ministry.
15. The presence of a counseling center of recovery and support activities at the church for singles and their children.
16. Institutional dollars to make the program viable.

Let's briefly look at each of these sixteen principles.

Theology of Humanity

The existing theology of humanity within the church is based on certain standards as normative. These standards are not exclusive to the church but have also been perpetrated by developmental psychology and society at large.

Dr. EmmaLou Benignus, in the keynote address at the Solo Flight Conference at Kanuga Conference Center in North Carolina, spoke of singleness as "the essential state."[1] Susan Muto, author of the book *Celebrating the Single Life,* speaks of singleness as the unique and onto-logical position—the end state that we will all finally achieve.[2] Bishop Johnson of North Carolina says, "We are all single. Some of us just happen to be married. That does not take away my singleness. We are singles who happen to live in units from time to time in our lives. If we submerge our individuality into relationships, we forget an important part of who we are."

Christian writer Harold Ivan Smith says that we all experience "seasons of singleness" in our lives.

Our theology of humanity must embrace singleness as a normative way of being in the world, must give recognition that the unmarried person has equal status in the eyes of God, and must be welcomed in the earthly kingdom as in the heavenly kingdom.

Perhaps as the basis for this theology of humanity we will begin with the fact that Jesus Christ was single, too.

Awareness and Support of Church Leadership

The senior pastor or rector of a church, regardless of its size, sets the tone for ministry.

If the pastor is accepting, welcoming, and inclusive, the leadership and the congregation will follow suit.

To point assistant ministers, lay leaders, and the congregation to the need for single-adult ministry and the opportunities in it, the senior pastor must first be informed of the issues of single life.

Senior pastors have ample opportunity to educate, inform, and support through their own actions, preaching, parish appointments and policies, and promotion.

At Christ Church Cathedral in Lexington, Kentucky, Dean Jim Burns translated an experience with singles into education, policy, and promotion. Early in his pastorate, an elderly parishioner told him that the parish "discriminated" against singles. The perplexed rector inquired what she meant. Her response: "For parish dinners, you advertise: families—$10; individuals—$7.50. That's discrimination!" Dean Burns took this information to the parish vestry; a new policy was established. Shortly thereafter, in sharing sponsorship of a particular ministry with another church, the dean was heard to say, "Wait! We'll have to make a change in the way these prices are set. We don't discriminate here—and this brochure says families—$15; individuals—$10."

The aware and informed senior pastor will know of suitable educational resources and will have those resources available. That pastor will seek full-time professional leadership for this ministry whenever possible. When resources are not available for full-time ministry, the pastor will work to include singles' ministry at some level of staff position, to emphasize its importance to the total life of the parish.

The sermons, informal actions, and words of the senior pastor will reflect a sensitivity to the inclusive theology of humanity and an insistence that this theology be upheld by staff and by resources provided in and for the parish.

One rector, discovering that a number of single adults congregate around the coffee pot following the 11:00 a.m. service each Sunday, makes a concentrated effort to stop by that spot for a visit. The simple gesture, requiring a few extra minutes out of a hectic Sunday schedule, reaps major results in terms of affirmation and relationship.

Another pastor offers a singles' "Love Liturgy" on the Sunday nearest Valentine's Day. "I know what a hard time many singles have with this secular day," he says. "The liturgy is built around the love passages from Scripture, such as 'love one another,' and emphasizes individual, not coupled, love."

These liturgies are statements to the lay leadership, the congregation, and single adults indicating that they are major, not minor, members of the parish.

Singles' Leadership and Leadership by Singles

Alla Renee-Campbell in her classic on grief recovery, *Life Is Goodbye,
Life Is Hello*, says that she feels one of the reasons her clients trust her to
go with them through the grief process is because she has *been* there.[3]
While it is certainly true that many gifted teachers and counselors are
able to take people through experiences and teach them well without
having lived a particular experience themselves, the actual living of an
experience gives a leader a different essential understanding that comes
only from life itself. As singles' leader Pat Jackard says, "Singleness is
part of the very fabric of my being."

People who have spent their adult lives living married or coupled
will find it very difficult to imagine what the lives of single people are
really like, in terms of advantages and disadvantages. Adults who have
been divorced or widowed and are remarried after at least a two- to five-
year period of singleness or those who have spent a number of adult
years being single prior to marriage will have a more immediate and in-
depth grasp of issues and great sensitivity. Tom Blackmon of Saint
Michael and All Angels Episcopal Church in Dallas believes the knowledge that the leader is now a single adult, or has lived a period of time as
a single adult, offers instant credibility within the singles' population.

It is important to note that singleness alone is not a sufficient credential for this leadership.

Among the more conservative churches, there seems to have been a
reluctance to hire leaders who are single. "It's not verbalized," said one
singles' consultant, "but the attitude is very entrenched. A person in
leadership has to embody the characteristics held up as 'ideal' for the
'Christian family.'" Yet it seems a contradiction in terms to offer a
ministry to single people, to speak of single as a wholesome, normal
option for life, and to hire a married person to lead the ministry.

A church that has based its ministry on an inclusive theology of
humanity will have single leaders in key leadership positions—on the
session, the vestry, teaching Sunday school, running the every member
canvass. As a counselor, one of the things I try to do is find models of
successful singleness for those persons who are struggling with the
concept of living a single life.

It is important for the self-esteem of the individuals involved, and for
the relevance of the ministry, that the leaders not only understand the

elements of the ministry and be trained to implement them, but also consider it a priority ministry. For this reason, it is preferable that the position of singles' leader not be combined with youth ministry or some other configuration that would limit the work.

While it is certainly better to have a person who works part time on singles' ministry than no one working in this area at all, both youth work and singles' work are complex and energy- and time-consuming. Different configurations of tasks might be more workable for part-time staff than combining these particular jobs.

A Mission Statement That Sets the Comprehensive Philosophy

While mission statements will require regular rethinking and adjustment or fine tuning in keeping with the necessary standard of flexibility, it is crucial to develop a basic statement that emphasizes: (1) community, friendship, support—not meeting and mating—as major goals of the ministry; (2) the spiritual component; (3) the evangelism component; (5) the nurturing-recovery component; (5) the balanced ministry component; and (6) the outreach, ecumenical, invitational nature of the ministry.

Some examples of mission statements are as follows:

ESP is an outreach ministry of Holy Innocents Church and invites single Atlantans into a holistic growth process. This process includes enhanced awareness and development of one's physical, intellectual, emotional, and spiritual life. ESP's objectives are to promote effective interaction and communication toward deepening relationships and to promote beneficial community projects.

Single Parents of Calvary are people who are seeking to strengthen themselves and their families through Christian fellowship, praise, prayer, and the proclamation of God's word.

Forty-Something Singles is a group that meets for fun, fellowship, spiritual growth, and community outreach. We welcome all singles age forty-plus from any faith.

Intergenerational Ministry to Single Adults is a place where single adults

from postcollege through postretirement can be in a safe and caring
community of people who understand and share issues, are involved in
life-long intellectual, spiritual, emotional, and physical growth, and wish
to promote effective interaction, communication, and service within the
parish, diocese, and community. Single adults of all faiths are welcome.

An Opportunity for Telling Stories and Listening

Telling stories and listening are important ingredients in singles' ministry
on several levels. As singles share their stories with other singles and
learn from one another, opportunities for healing and growth abound.
Neither the church nor the secular community provides many models of
successful singleness. In the telling of personal stories, singles pass on
coping skills, attitudes, philosophies, and theologies for life as a single
person.

As the larger parish community listens, stereotypes can be broken
down. Singles have stereotypes of singles and of married people. Married people have stereotypes of married relationships and of singles. As
structured opportunities for telling and hearing stories are provided, there
can be a better understanding both intergroup and intragroup.

Flexibility in Dealing with a Flexible Population

Virtually all singles' leaders agree that flexibility is a key ingredient for
singles' ministry. Said one leader, "If you are the kind of person who
wants to get a 'formula' down for a program and not worry about it
anymore, singles' ministry is not for you. Flexibility is the name of the
game. You have to be able to go with the flow; be sensitive to your
current population, even if it shifts in midyear, and your carefully made
plans are all out the window."

The singles' population is constantly changing. Some label that shift
"unstable." People move, remarry, or marry for the first time. In fact,
singles, often considered mobile, can be targeted as corporate transients,
moved around the country by employers who find it easier to move an
"unattached" individual than a family. Singles are, indeed, subject to
demographic change. A "season of singleness" may be a year for one

person, months for another, and a lifetime for yet another. And status may change unexpectedly.

Psychotherapist John Stathas, coordinator of singles' ministry at Holy Innocents Episcopal Church in Atlanta, says that he spends a good portion of his time counseling single adults considering marriage or re-marriage, getting into a relationship, or ending one.

A person's single state may not be the only indicator of that person's interest in singles' activities. Some singles are interested in organized activities when they are not involved in a romantic relationship; when they are "dating" regularly, they aren't on the scene. This is simply a fact of life in the singles' world. It is not a criterion for whether or not the ministry is "good."

Another flexibility factor concerns life transitions particular to singles. Singles have the usual life transitions of all human beings—passing milestone birthdays, loss of parents, children graduating or marrying, their own divorces, death of spouses, remarriages, second divorces, moving into complete aloneness when all children are gone from the home.

Other life transitions might go unrecognized in the world at large. All parents experience the empty nest syndrome to some degree when each child leaves home, and with an increased intensity when the last child is gone. For coupled homes, this marks the time when the adult partners must again face each other without the buffer of children—an experience fraught with its own difficulties. For the parent who has been single for a number of years and has felt "adjusted" to that reality, there is suddenly the new reality of *total* aloneness for the first time. This experience can often cause a period of renewed stress for even the "re-covered" single parent. A similar experience is caused by the death of parents with whom a single-adult "child" has been living and for whom that child has been primary caretaker. As one such child expressed it, "My whole world stopped. There *is* no one else in it." This situation is especially intense if the child happens to be the only child or the only remaining child in a family.

Age milestones may carry a great degree of significance for the single in relation to family and societal expectations. Singles approach-ing thirty are extremely aware that their families are becoming restless about whether or not they will have grandchildren soon, whether the young man or young woman is becoming interested in a career to the detriment of finding a husband or wife. The approach of the thirties marks a turning point—one about which many in this age group are made to feel uneasy. As one single pointed out, every telephone call from her parents begins with the hopeful question, "Any good news yet?" in reference to her dating life.

If the single woman is approaching forty, she may be concerned about the ticking of her biological clock. Women of this age are also aware with each decade that the odds for marriage or remarriage are against them. These types of issues, of course, are simply added to those that all people address around such milestone birthdays. At present no studies have looked scientifically at how single adults, as opposed to coupled adults, manage the passages or transitions of their lives. Such studies as Gail Sheehy's *Passages* are, like developmental psychology, based on the assumption that at a certain age people marry and live out their lives from that perspective. So, while scientific information is not available at this time, experience of those who work with single individuals shows that there are differences as well as similarities in both crisis and transition situations. Awareness of developments and research in this area is important for those involved in pastoral care.

Indeed, Harold Ivan Smith, an internationally known singles' consultant and lecturer in Kansas City is involved in research as to how the single adult faces death and how that might differ from the experience of one who is coupled or married. According to Smith, some of the issues that arise in counseling single adults about death (in addition to "normal" grief issues) include no family support while going through the experience, the fear of no family to care for the single adult as death approaches, fear no one will be there during the death process, the possibility of no family burial plot or place to be buried, fear that no one will remember or miss them, plus issues extending from divorce.[4]

Sensitivity in Naming of Programs and Activities

There seem to be two distinct philosophies of naming programs and activities for single adults.

1. Some form of the term *single* is used in program titles to indicate that these offerings are geared for those who are not currently married.

2. No derivative of the term *single* or its synonyms is used, as single individuals may be sensitive to this form of identification. This sensitivity points to societal norms and resultant pressures on the nonmarried person.

One young woman was quoted, "I hate that [singles] label! It hasn't been a concern of mine. It isn't a concern of mine. It just doesn't have anything to do with my life!" This twenty-five-year-old went on to say, "I'm not ready for marriage right now, like a lot of people my age." She maintained that she is "not interested in bar hopping," or, at the other end of the spectrum, support groups. "Anything labeled 'single' is just not of interest to me." Singles' leaders need to be aware that this attitude is possible from singles of all ages who find the terminology pejorative rather than demographic.

The immediate postcollege, never-married age group seems to prefer titles for programs and activities that express an attitude from the church as welcoming "those who aren't perfect," titles that have an upbeat and challenging connotation. One group of twenty-something to thirty-something singles chose the name Saints and Sinners for their Bible study group. Their second choice was New Directions.

For groups or activities that relate to recovery there might be different names than for those more general in orientation.

Groups that choose to use the name or concept of singleness in their titles feel this is important in overcoming the idea that there is something "abnormal" about singleness; they point to parallel activities for youth, men, and women that clearly delineate the target population.

Like any other segment of the population, singles will have divergent views on this subject; personal responses will vary.

Clearly, there is a need to stay away from titles that indicate sadness or rejection or a focus on dating and mating. Members of one group interviewed recalled an early name: Saint S—'s Single Hearts. An upswing in attendance began when the name of the group was changed. The idea is to attract individuals to the program or activity by using a name that (1) speaks to the target population and (2) motivates and inspires participation.

The following samples of names have been used successfully: High Point, an ongoing Baptist singles' ministry; Single Mingle, an activity sponsored by High Point, clearly indicating a social gathering; Just

Friends, an Episcopal dinner-social group; Singularly Significant, an
Episcopal Sunday school class; The Source, an interdenominational
singles' organization devoted to smaller parishes unable to establish their
own individual singles' ministry; Oasis, divorce/grief support groups;
Solo Flight, divorce recovery/other singles' activities. Other names
include Kindred Spirits, Common Ground, AND TNT Singles.

Understanding the Needs of the Current Population

Knowing the prevailing issues of the target population is critical to the
success of any program. The finest singles' social program in town will
not draw participants if the major need of the population is divorce recovery and single-parenting issues. Singles' leaders have devoted much
time and energy to discovering the needs of the singles' population. The
following list is a composite of information gathered at Montreat (Presbyterian) Conference Center and Kanuga (Episcopal) Conference Center.
Those persons surveyed ranged in age from twenty-eight to seventy-six
and were residents of New York, Pennsylvania, Connecticut, Ohio,
Arizona, Texas, North Carolina, South Carolina, Virginia, Tennessee,
Georgia, Alabama, and Kentucky. The needs are listed in order of
priority as reported by these two populations.

Needs:
1. Personal wholeness
2. Singles' spirituality
3. Singles' sexuality
4. Singles' activities that offer opportunities for networking
   across parish lines

Ways of meeting those needs:
5. A national denominational communique, network for singles
6. Leadership training in singles' work for clergy and lay leaders
7. Workshops, support groups on loneliness
8. Leadership training for singles who wish to establish programs
   within their churches
9. Workshops and support groups on relationship dependency
10. Workshops and support groups on loneliness crutches

11. Workshops and support groups on life transitions
12. Advocacy training for singles
13. Workshops and support groups on single parenting
14. Workshops and support groups on grief recovery
15. Sunday school classes for singles
16. Workshops and support groups on divorce recovery
17. Workshops and support groups for children of divorce
18. Social activities and/or companionship opportunities
19. Network for dating people with shared values through church channels

Singles' Sunday School Class

While many large Protestant churches have historically divided their adult Christian education offerings by gender or age categories, Episcopal, Presbyterian, and Lutheran churches have not practiced such divisions to any great degree. Adult education may, at best, involve one large "pastor's forum" and possibly a few smaller special interest groups, depending on the size of the parish.

For many single persons, walking into a large adult gathering on Sunday morning, especially if they are new to the church, is a painful prospect. The entire assemblage, singles say, seems to have "coupled" written across its face. People appear to sit as couples and relate to other couples.

The Rev. Mike Lumpkin speaks emphatically from his own experience as a single: "If you haven't ever walked into one of those church gatherings as an adult single, don't knock it. You just don't know how it feels!"

If you are establishing a singles' Sunday school class, remember, all singles will not want or need singles' activities, just as all youth do not want youth activities. This is *not* an indication that the parish does not need the ministry. A certain number of single people may be the greatest stumbling block to establishment of a ministry, declaring, "I'm okay. I have a very full life and just don't understand what you're talking about." One man, after months of this kind of resistance, enrolled in the singles' Sunday school class "to help you people out." The constant defense of his own posture in lieu of participation in the class finally brought other class members to say, "Why don't *you* go to another class? We want *this* one!"

The number one reason for offering a singles' Sunday school class is to provide an accessible point of entry for singles who might otherwise feel intimidated by the coupledness they perceive in the parish.

The fact that a singles' class exists makes a statement to those who look at the parish offerings: This is a place where singles can find others who understand their lifestyle, who might share some ideas and life experiences.

The possibility for discussions relating spiritual issues to daily life will be particularly important to some singles. Others may find the regular offerings of the parish more to their liking. Ideally, it will not be an either/or but a both/and situation.

Networking

One request heard repeatedly is that single people within the church want to meet other single people. In an article written for the Diocese of Central New York following the first Solo Flight Conference, authors Carole George and Marcia Lawrence wrote: "Everyone agreed that the best part of the conference was the opportunity to network with other singles . . . to discover how they manage their lives . . . to share that experience."[5]

Once a network begins, individuals will travel considerable distances to participate in activities. This clearly indicates that many singles are hungry for companionship that has a shared spiritual base.

While there is an acknowledged and entirely understandable need among this population to meet potential mates who share their values, the greater need is for companionship, for identifying other persons who might be available to enjoy activities or simply spend time together, and for learning from others who have traveled similar paths. For this is an area of life about which little has been written. Carolyn Koons reports that while doing research for *Single Adult Passages* she went to the largest library in Southern California. This library houses books for eight universities. While walking through with the research librarian, Koons discovered that there were three floors of books on human development and psychology, but there were only four books that had material about singles, other than the volumes on divorce recovery.

Single individuals are learning from other singles how to live creatively, constructively, contentedly, and productively in a world planned around married and coupled people. An active network is an important component of this discovery process.

Having a Balanced Ministry

Spiritual, emotional, intellectual, physical, social—all five aspects are important in developing a singles' ministry. It may not be possible to begin all five aspects of ministry simultaneously. Where to begin? The answer depends on the needs in a specific parish. Yet a program that is purely social and neglects the spiritual aspects of life will fail, as will the purely spiritual program that fails to take into account the emotional or recovery aspects and personal growth of participants—the need to continue learning and giving throughout life. Developing a balanced mission statement and keeping in constant check with the statement will help keep a ministry on track.

Publicity: Frequent, Well Done, Upbeat, Personal

No program will be successful without publicity. Publicity is communication—a way of letting the target population know what is available to them in a strong but not intrusive way. Communication will take place in several forms:

1. Direct communication via letter to individuals
2. Group/bulk mailings of newsletters, brochures, etc.
3. General brochures and calendars in tract rack at the church
4. Announcements in general church bulletins, newsletters, and diocesan/regional publications
5. Special mailings, public announcements
6. Telephone networks
7. Birthday, holiday, support mailings, and communiques.

Each type of communication has its place and its importance. Direct mailings or letters offer an opportunity for personal notes with reference to specific needs or interests of which the director may be aware. Such mailings make each individual feel special, cared for. Group/bulk mailings of singles' newsletters and calendars are regularly scheduled opportunities for learning about what is available. Placing general brochures about the nature of the ministry and calendars of events in the tract rack of the church provides newcomers easy access to information. Announcements in general mailings of the parish and regional publications of the denomination inform the larger singles' community that may wish to take part in activities; these avenues also help educate the general population in regard to singles. Special mailings and special announcements are particularly helpful when an event is open to the general public. Telephone networks and specialized mailings for birthdays, special anniversaries, holidays, or support purposes individualize the ministry and encourage a sense of family support within the community.

A Council of Single People

The establishment of a singles' council within a parish will bring together leaders responsible for all phases of the ministry, providing them an opportunity to work together under the mission statement for the whole ministry and the whole church. A singles' council also provides opportunity for a more holistic and organic approach to ministry, with each person seeing the whole and the sum of the parts. It gives the director and professional staff a back-up team and spreads the base of responsibility for the ministry.

Core of Individuals Taking Ownership

A core group of leaders and involved members who regularly attend functions is essential to the health and well being of the ministry. This nucleus will offer diverse and energetic leadership, with opportunities for both continuity and change. Professional staff can assist, empowering, assessing, and providing vision.

A Counseling Center of Recovery and Support Activities at the Church

While singles' ministry is about much more than brokenness or recovery, the work of divorce and grief recovery are major components of any singles' ministry program. Programs meeting crisis needs—be they emotional, spiritual, or financial—of the suddenly single and their families need to be easily accessible. Individual and group counseling, from pastoral counseling to therapy, in the safe and familiar context of the parish, should be available. Beyond that which is available through the parish itself, singles' directors should provide updated lists of effective resources in the key areas of crisis. Consider giving "scholarship" money to those who cannot afford counseling.

Investing Institutional Dollars in the Ministry

The most successful singles' ministry programs are, by and large, part of the operating budget of particular parishes. The investment of institutional dollars makes a church accountable for the work; it gives it importance in the eyes of the parish; it says to singles, "You are a major part of the life of this church."

Successful programs cannot exist without funds. Jim Smoke, a leading author on singles' issues, says, "To exist as a recognized ministry in the church, both physical facilities and budgeting monies must be generously invested. This can no longer be a 'broom closet operation.'" Real ministries cost real monies.[6]

When parish leadership is approached for funding, it is not unusual to hear someone say, "We had a group like that ten years ago and it disappeared. Must not need it!"

In most cases ministries born out of short-term personal need and headed by volunteers without institutional support in terms of both monies and staff will eventually die out due to a number of factors: lack of overall vision and plan, changes in volunteer needs or singles' population, and exhaustion of volunteer leaders who feel themselves pushing boulders uphill without institutional support.

A commitment of institutional monies to staffing and program gives single-adult ministry the opportunity to develop a vision and plan that will not only speak to current needs, but will also anticipate the future and continue all-important leadership training and networking with other singles' leadership.

Answered Questions

In Chapter II the question was raised "What is singles' ministry?" In story, in principle, and in process, the definition is revealed. Single-adult ministry is *not* a loosely affiliated, volunteer-run social service where society's misfits and losers come together in desperate need of dates or mates. Rather, it is the pivot on which a new theology turns in the church—a theology with broad-reaching implications for the future of the whole church and society.

CHAPTER V

Into the New Century: Implications for the Future

Futurists tell us that by the year 2000, fifty-two percent of the population of the United States over the age of twenty-five will be single.[1] Economic conditions as well as feelings of personal isolation will make new configurations in living more the norm than the exception. "The Golden Girls" and "Three's Company" may well be more model than amusement.

Pastors and congregations across the country look toward this new century with the knowledge that it has never been more crucial for the church to be what it claims to be—the household of God, the family of Christ.

But there must be no confusion.

The family of God is not, nor has it ever been, a nuclear family—mother, father, 2.2 children, picket fence, Norman Rockwell Thanksgiving scene.

The members of Christ's family are many and diverse, and they have grown in diverse, unanticipated, and often uncomfortable directions during this twentieth century.

Today's "family tables" find single fathers, divorced sisters, widowed aunts and their lovers, stepbrothers and sisters, homosexual sons and daughters, unmarried friends seated together in unlikely tableau, seeking communion and community.

So also does the table of our Lord.

The stories of Randy and Carol and Jimmy and Allison are the stories of people already in the pews and many more people just outside the church doors. In churches such as Saint Michael and All Angels, Calvary, Prairie Village, Holy Innocents, Christ Church Cathedral, and others like them, the response has begun.

What are the implications for the future?

Reexamining a Theology of Humanity

The church must reexamine its theology of humanity and manifestations of that theology in terms of symbolism, language, program, and attitude and know how the unmarried person is excluded or marginalized.

Certainly a philosophy of the wholeness of the body of Christ is theologically consistent and correct.

As Janet Grant of Lutheran-Episcopal Center in Minneapolis says in addressing the subject of single-adult ministry: "I really don't believe in single-adult ministry or any other subgroup ministry. But to believe the need for such subgroup ministries will disappear in my lifetime is totally unrealistic."

Grant has tapped into a fundamental sociological and psychological reality, an ageless human truth: People do group. Left to their own devices, human beings seek units in which they feel welcomed, comfortable, and nurtured, groups in which values, joys, and sorrows are shared. Ban Greek-letter sororities and fraternities from a college campus and secret societies and other named groups will evolve. Church youth groups, men's groups, and women's groups speak to this same basic need. There may be overlap among groups. There may be a sense of belonging to the larger unit. But the need to have a more intimate circle is there.

For those singles who may have no family close by, this subgrouping of the church, which shares the essence of the state of beingness of this particular period of life, may truly be "family." For others, it is a place of going and doing, a place of entry into the larger body of the church.

This larger body has for many years acted out and spoken in the language of the perceived prevailing culture—the nuclear family. We've seen parish bulletins that announce Valentine's Day renewal of marriage vows with no thought of an alternative offering for singles; we've heard sermons on the marriage/divorce gospel with no plan for dealing with the response from the pews, no person assigned to do an emotional/spiritual follow-up with either adults or children. There are stories of the youth worker who naively asked a class of teens if any of them knew "anyone" who was divorced, only to discover that everyone in the class came from a divorced family. Advertisements for "family dinners," foyer groups, or cell groups structured for six, eight, or ten people, implying coupledness. In general, the church has provided no symbol and ritual to recognize and support the estate of singleness.

Lawrence Bottom, a black Presbyterian theologian from Atlanta, re-
flected on this phenomena during a singles' conference in North Carolina. "It would seem that the church would figure out that these things
are the same. But no, we have to deal with blacks, then with women,
then with gays, and now with singles. It's all the same. Exclusiveness.
Discrimination."

For generations American society has viewed the nuclear family as a
standard and anything outside of it as deviant. Those who live outside of
the standard are looked upon as substandard or as living only partial
lives. So powerful is the conditioning that persons outside the nuclear
family standard are made to consider themselves as pale imitations of a
greater reality, waiting in the wings for completion through an other, or
having passed their time of completion, now to live their lives incom-
pletely.

In an institution committed to following the great commandment
"Love one another as I have loved you" (John 15:12), it is time to open
ourselves to the possibility that there are other ways to understand and
live out this commandment than the nuclear family—other ways to see
ourselves and one another, other ways to take care of ourselves and one
another. Edging toward the fifty-two percent mark as a portion of the
overall population, singles have quietly begun to create new ways of
living in this society—home sharing, group housing, roommates—building communities of concern and companionship in the largeness, the
coldness of the world. Nearing the day when the single population will
not only meet but pass the fifty-two percent marker, we *must* look at the
very real possibility that new configurations of human beings—friends,
companions, colleagues—may also prove to be foundational units in
society, other models of living into the commandment to "love one
another."

Bishop Craig Anderson, formerly of South Dakota now Dean of
General Theological Seminary, works for the rights of Native Americans
and for the full participation of women in the Episcopal Church. His
statement is compelling for all: "We must talk about a theology of
humanity that doesn't have to reinvent the wheel every time we turn
around—that speaks to the whole people of God."

Educating the Church

A second implication of the future predictions is that if we are to minister to whole people—single or married—the church must be prepared to educate, providing a comprehensive, integrated curriculum that begins in the earliest years.

Psychologist Dorothy Corkhill Briggs in her book *Your Child's Self Esteem;* Virginia Satir, the late family therapist and author of *People-making*; and the state of California, in a ground-breaking study on the health and wholeness of human beings—all speak to the development of positive feelings about self as basic to wellness. In the way both church and society have of overkilling a word or concept, turning it into a buzz-word and then discarding it without any sense of integrated learning, *self-esteem* seems on the way "out" of vocabularies and good graces.

But self-esteem and personal wholeness are key in developing a life-long learning curriculum for the church based on the theology of human-ity that understands that "married" is not the paradigm on which all human development rests. To teach as if it were so is to invite problems that require extensive recovery ministry, teaching that we are not two-by-two on the way to the ark; we do not require a partner to stand upright and live fully.

Research is just beginning to work toward production of develop-mental charts based on a single rather than a married model. These charts will not replace traditional models but supplement our knowledge concerning the real lives of real human beings. Infancy. Childhood. Adolescence. Teen age. College/first job. ??? The new chart will re-cognize that marriage is not a *given* at any stage of life. This recognition and recharting may well produce ground-breaking new information as to how adult single people move through the middle and late years of their lives.

With this understanding comes the realization that a word looms large in lives not prepared for living into it. The word is *loneliness*. Both Billy Graham and Mother Teresa have called loneliness the single greatest affliction in modern life.

The church is uniquely equipped to address this issue from cradle to grave—to develop within its curriculum positive experiences of solitude as well as community. Times when, as one bishop says, we noisy souls can "shut up and listen"—to God.

When I was a child, during hot southern summers, my sisters and I were required to go to our rooms for an hour or so during the heat of noonday. We did not have to go to sleep. We could read, write, play quietly. But we were to be by ourselves, apart from our friends, apart from activity, apart from the rest of the household, apart from the outside world. I recall how we fought the appointed time. Dim recollections of electric fans whirring, pages turning, a window seat—feelings of peace, quiet, rest.

But the experience was of infinite value in my own adjustment to singleness—a powerful internal knowing that alone is okay, alone can be both full and good, alone does not have to be scary or avoided at all costs—even when the cost is destructive and inappropriate relationships. This knowledge is integrally connected to the idea that I am personally whole . . . enough . . . sufficient . . . in and of myself, without an other. Only God.

These concepts must be built into the fabric of young lives inundated by the drone of television and Muzak and people. They must be built into day-care centers and preschools where teachers are trained to develop such "okayness." In youth camps and retreats and conferences that teach silence, being alone, wilderness survival skills—emotional and physical as well as spiritual. In young adult, mid-adult, and older-adult classes and retreats in which the experience of alone, of emptying out, of centering down are taught and encouraged and enjoyed so that alone is not filled with terrible pain and fear.

This kind of integrated, life-long learning is not "borrowing from behavioral science," but rather, combining knowledge of both the spiritual and the emotional to open lives to true wholeness and health.

Rethinking Outreach

The church must also rethink its "missionary and outreach" work to include the new poor—the newly marginalized, as well as those who suffer in third-world countries and city ghettos. Single parents are regularly faced with lack of job skills and/or low-paying jobs, insufficient or nonexistent benefits (particularly for women), lack of child-care facilities, insufficient housing, struggles with general well-being, quality of life and overall fatigue, and no retirement plans. These are not issues limited to inner cities; they are alive and well in middle-class suburbs and middle-class churches. This is not an "occasional happening" to be handled by the minister's discretionary fund but an oft-repeated theme. Special funds, day-care centers, job banks, skills training—these are only a few of the ministries churches might offer to help an ever-growing segment of the population; many of these people, to the surprise of most churches, already live in embarrassed silence on the church roles.

New Theological Insights for Teaching

New theological insights are needed that provide scripturally based teaching on issues of singleness, including divorce, remarriage, singles' sexuality, sperm-donor babies, single-parent adoptions, shared living arrangements, AIDS, and homosexuality. As more children of divorce move into adulthood, additional emergent issues will command the attention of the church. Many singles have suffered needlessly from Scripture taken out of context, from Scripture misinterpreted or misused. Faced with life issues that may not be familiar to them, or to their churches, singles are searching for answers to profound questions. It is past time for these questions to be seriously considered in the light of the Gospel.

Training Clergy

Emerging and existing clergy must be trained in concepts of singles' ministry through seminary coursework in the area of pastoral theology, field work in clinical pastoral education, continuing education seminars, mentor relationships, and trainer courses. Resources are just beginning to be developed. Perhaps the greatest human resources to date are people working in the field who can provide the benefit of on-the-job experience to assist seminaries and other training programs in this all-important field.

Such an educational program will call for a willingness on the part of academia to welcome into classrooms outsiders who have experience and training in singles' ministry. The numbers of single adults in the population warrant immediate and serious attention from any institution or group that is training for ministry.

Embracing Opportunities in Spirituality

The church must embrace the opportunity for deeper experiences of God available in the single life.

Facing life alone as a single adult confronts humans with profound life questions.

In divorce-recovery work I list working priorities as (1) the internal self, (2) the functional self, and (3) the social self, while acknowledging that most people reverse that order until, pushed to the limits of their endurance and having exhausted all other resources, they admit that just *maybe* it is time to look inside the self—to look at God.

Single adults have, like the rest of society, been programmed since birth to expect to move into the married state in young adulthood and to live in that state for many years. Despite divorce statistics and statistics concerning later ages for marriage, the myth persists, bringing spiritual, societal, and emotional/developmental pressures on the single individual. To recognize this reality is also to recognize the death and resurrection motif in the single life.

Whether the death is of marriage, spouse, dreams, or life expectations, there is a necessary letting go and hearing God's call for this particular season of life. This experience brings many single individuals face to face with ultimate questions, unbuffered and unsupported by the energy and intimacy of a committed relationship.

In the face of a society and, yes, a church that "affirm" with such messages as, "Oh, you're so pretty! You know you'll be married (or married again) soon!" or, "There are plenty of women just waiting for a man like you!" singles speak to themselves in their own aloneness:

"What does my life mean if I am to live it alone? If I am not/no longer a wife/husband? If I never have children?"

"Does God really mean for me to live by myself for the rest of my life? Why?"

"Why does it feel so empty? Why am I so scared? Why won't the hunger go away?"

"Can I be happy without a mate?"

The journey from these questions to self-affirmation in life as a single person uniquely created by God is not an easy one. There is sadness, fear, anger, and loneliness.

And there is the incredible grace of opportunity to move from loneliness into solitude and in that solitude to encounter the mysterious and all-encompassing relationship with God, which fills the emptiness, feeds the hunger, heals the fear, as no earthly relationship can.

There's the incredible grace of opportunity to know life more truly whole than ever imagined. To live the experience of transfiguration and transcendence.

It is to this journey that I believe the church is called to minister.

Each aspect of the ministry is but a step on the journey—each aspect speaking to individuals, extending the hand of God, as they need to experience its touch at that moment.

There is no way to know when the all-powerful love of God will touch a heart and soul. It may come in the embraces of a divorce recovery group, holding a weeping brother.

It may come in the comfortable companionship around a Sunday brunch table.

It may come as the cup is passed during communion at a singles' retreat.

If we build it—they *will* come . . . and move toward the wholeness of God's love.

Summary

Recently National Public Radio's "Morning Edition" reported on a Chicago ministry coming out of a "new kind of church." Its focus: the Latino population of the city; taking AIDS education into the high schools, providing that education in sermons as well as counseling situations; teaching struggling single mothers that the Gospel message of love has to do with self-respect, that boundaries are a part of that message, that emotional abuse is not acceptable. This ministry, said the announcer, is "moving into the heart of loneliness to teach; asking what messages are being given the rising generation."

The stories have a familiar ring. They are true not just among ethnic populations in crowded cities, but also in suburbs and apartment complexes and neighborhoods all across the face of America.

The greater truth must be a "new kind of church" that in its beingness and its doingness truly lives the words: "very members incorporate in the mystical body of thy Son, the blessed company of *all* faithful people."[2]

Defusing Stereotypes: Group Designs

Time Allotted: One three-hour session or three one-hour sessions.

Hour/Session One: Definitions

Format: Participants in small groups.

Equipment: Pencils and paper, flip chart or chalkboard.

Facilitator's Role: Brief introduction concerning how our personal experiences impact the way we define and understand words. Write the following words on the board:

> *single   married   divorced   widowed   separated*
> *never-married   bachelor*

Directions: Have each participant define the words on paper and then read the definitions to the small group. Each group is responsible for coming up with a group definition of one of the words (or two each, if there are not enough groups) and sharing the definition with the large group, posting the definition on newsprint or a chalkboard. In small groups participants should compare their individual definitions to those presented to the large group and further discuss where the various definitions come from.

Hour/Session Two: Stereotypes

Format: Participants in small groups.

Equipment: Pencils and paper, flip chart or chalkboard.

Facilitator's Role: Brief introduction concerning stereotypes and how our life experiences impact the stereotypes we hold of people.

Write the following on newsprint or chalkboard:

> *Singles always* _____
> *Divorced people always* _____
> *Widowed people always* _____
> *Married people always* _____
> *Couples always* _____

For each phrase ask each participant to write down the first thing that comes to mind.

Directions: After participants have filled in the blanks, have them discuss their "answers" with the small group. Each group should report to the large group, relating the stereotypes.

Hour/Session Three: Updating Information

Format: Participants in small groups.

Equipment: Pencils and paper, flip chart or chalkboard.

Facilitator's Role: Short talk about how we can get locked into old information and can't get away from it, even when it is outdated and no longer useful. Use an example from life, such as "When I was growing up, my father told me that nice girls did not talk to boys on street corners. Now, as a grown woman, if I happen to be talking to a man on a corner, I always have this urge to move toward the center of the block." You may use this story or one from your own experience.

Present the following thought process based on principles of Transactional Analysis, as used by Dr. Pearl Rutledge, counseling psychologist, concerning irrational and rational behavior.

Old message:
Nice girls don't talk to boys on street corners.

Reactive/irrational behavior: If talking to a man on street corner, feel need to move to center of block.

Filter old messages:
What is wrong/outdated about each old message?

How can I update and get new messages?
1. I am not a girl; I am a woman.
2. The act of talking on a street corner is not in itself bad.
3. I am capable of deciding where it is appropriate to talk to people.

Proactive/rational behavior based on updated messages: I will choose to have conversations with a person of choice, in a locale of choice, without feelings of guilt.

Directions: Ask participants to write down two old messages they are aware they have in their lives:

1. On any topic
2. Concerning married and single people

In small groups participants should discuss their old messages, filter them, and write down updated information they have received on the subject during these sessions.

Participants should write down how rational behavior will emerge from the updated messages and what that new behavior might be.

Facilitator's Role: Remind participants of the five stereotypes discussed in Session Two. Lead a discussion in which the group adapts examples from those five stereotypes to the rational/irrational behavior model discussed in this hour.

A Rationale
for Single-Adult Ministry

Presented to the Vestry of Christ Church Cathedral
Lexington, Kentucky
(Reprinted with permission.)

To the Vestry of Christ Church Cathedral

I believe that as Christians we are called to bring others to Christ; to know ourselves that the only true wholeness is in and through Him; to make that truth real in the lives of others through the witness of our lives and the commitment of our hearts; to be the community of believers whose faith makes a difference in how we think and speak and act and live.

As a human being and as a therapist, I know that there are times in every life when the stark realities of problems and of pain obscure the available truth and the possible wholeness. In those times, few words can reach the mind or heart of a struggler; practical help which speaks to human needs from a foundation of faith offers a statement of faith which is dimly perceived during the actual crisis, often recognized and embraced as God's hand in retrospect.

With these simple words as background, I offer you the following information concerning an area of ministry which is involved with a journey toward wholeness not often recognized by the church. The segmenting by categories is for the sake of awareness; of definition; of clarification—not for the sake of segregation. It is my belief that as we are aware of the truth of the lives of others beside ourselves, we can be more truly inclusive, integrated, and whole than when we have not ourselves lived an experience, and cannot feel it in its depths.

I hope you will consider prayerfully the following pages . . .

Categories of Single Persons

1. Young singles (in their twenties).
   Have finished their schooling, are in their first job, and most
   have not married.

2. Middle singles (thirties, forties, early fifties).
   A. Divorced:
      Recently: in grief/recovery (months, several years—depending
      on length of separation, settlement issues, etc.).

      Divorced:
      Dealing with ongoing issues of custody, finance, etc.
      Divorce issues settled; ongoing single issues predominate.

   B. Never married:
      Often quite comfortable financially; many feel they "don't fit
      in" most of society.

   C. Widowed:
      Recently; in grief/recovery (months, several years—depending
      on numerous issues).

      Widowed:
      Widowed for a number of years and not remarried.

3. Older singles.
   A. Divorced: recently (see above).

      Divorced: for a number of years (see above).

      Divorce for older singles frequently carries more guilt issues.

   B. Never married (see above).

   C. Widowed: recently (see above).

      Widowed: for a number of years (see above).

How do categories correlate with needs?

There are seven categories listed above. Each of the seven has needs that
are distinctly different from the other six, as well as shared ideas of need.

History of Singles' Ministry at Christ Church, 1980-1990

How has singles' ministry been defined in this and other parishes?

Primarily as a self-generated group which comes together for periodic social functions, sometimes combined with church services, or liturgical seasons.

Who has been "in charge" of singles' ministry?

In general, the work of singles' ministry has gone forth under the direction of lay people who feel called for a length of time to initiate a program for singles. One or more of the clergy offer guidance and support as requested.

How has this worked?

The lay person in charge generally represents a group of single individuals who share an area of need and want to meet other single individuals within the church with similar needs. Social activities and/or programs of service and study which correspond to the needs and personality of the current leader prevail for a period of time. When the capacity for carrying the burden of leadership has been exhausted, the effort dies out, to be resurrected again in the same manner.

Why, if there IS such a need, has there been no sustained effort?

1.   One-track planning cannot meet diverse needs.

2.   Planning from personal *neediness*, as opposed to carefully thought out need, is generally doomed.

3.   Nowhere in the regular printed material for this parish is there any indication that the world of single people is a recognized priority for this parish—in any of the basic seven areas of category and need.

4.   Our lack of statement makes a statement.

Have we looked to the diocese and national church for guidance and direction?

National church. There is no desk or office at the national level that is responsible for work in the area of singles' ministry. The Commission on Human Affairs of the Church has asked to be kept apprised of any work in this area which goes forth on the local level.

Diocesan. In March of 1990, an article in *The Advocate* entitled "Ministry to Singles," written by Lucyle Stanley, brought a ground swell of reaction from across the nation. As a result of this article, a Task Force on Singles' Ministry was formed with three purposes in mind: (1) To identify types and numbers of single persons in the Diocese of Lexington. (2) To offer a diocesan-wide intergenerational function for single people. (3) To present a resolution to the Diocesan Convention to form a department or commission that would make this work a permanent part of the structure of this diocese. Bishop Wimberly has recognized the successful completion of these tasks by appointing a body on singles' ministry, to be named by the Executive Council as either department or commission.

If we have no guidance nationally, what have we learned, and how?

Locally, we have learned from other churches, of other denominations:

In Central Kentucky, the Baptist Church offers the most complete ministry for single persons. This ministry includes:

1. A staff person in the parish—clergy and/or lay—whose major job focus is singles' ministry.

2. Regular, ongoing activities sponsored by the church as a part of its ministry.

3. In many cases, a special facility and special Christian education efforts for single persons.

4. Regular paid advertisements in the local newspaper, separate from the usual church ads, which allow the community to know that these churches recognize particular areas of need and attempt to help.

From other dioceses we have learned of particular parishes which have successful programs.

1. The focus is intentional, and has program and staff support, as well as

2. Good lay leadership.

3. Generally works in interest modules.

4. Frequently joins with other groups—primarily Presbyterian, Lutheran, Roman Catholic, occasionally Methodist or Dis ciples.

5. Advertise.

From our own diocese we have learned:

1. One hundred and five individuals—men and women ranging in age from twenty-three to eighty—attended the first Inter-generational Singles' Event last September.

2. For every single man or woman who is comfortable and satisfied with their life in their church, there are ten to twelve or more who feel left out, different, unimportant.

3. Younger singles are growing through their young adulthood with these feelings; many middle and older singles are finding these feelings coming upon them when they are "suddenly single" and, after years of feeling comfortable in family-oriented churches, know a different reality in their new lives.

4. There is a great need for the church at large to recognize that:

    SINGLE IS NOT a victim state.

    SINGLE IS NOT necessarily a temporary state.

    SINGLE IS NOT a lesser state.

    SINGLE IS NOT a threatening state.

    SINGLE IS a growing state.

SINGLE IS NOT going away.

SINGLES GO wherever they find a religious body which recognizes their needs—even if they have to go outside their own denomination.

Ministries for Singles at Christ Church as of January 1991

"Just Friends"

Convener: Helen Adkinson

"Just Friends" is the 1990-91 edition of the singles' group "Cathedral Single Hearts" started at Christmas of 1989. The format is much the same: the group gathers at someone's home one weekend night a month, or plans an excursion. Some trips have been to a Red's ball game and to Comedy on Broadway. One Wednesday night a month the group has dinner at a nearby restaurant following the 5:15 P.M. eucharist. "Just Friends" was chosen as the name to indicate that dating and mating were *not* the purposes, and to encourage the participation of nonsingle persons who might be interested. The age range of this group is thirty to thirty-five, with a few individuals outside ranging on either end of the spectrum.

"Looking into Divorce with the Eyes of Faith"

Teacher: Kay Collier-Slone

A three-session series of classes offered free of charge during the first three weeks of September. Average attendance at the class was six. Announcement for these classes ran in the *Advocate, Cathedral Calling* (was too late for *Evangel*), and in the "Church Notes" in the local newspaper. Participants represented the Presbyterian, Roman Catholic and Methodist churches, as well as Episcopal. Presbyterians predominated.

* * * * *

Offerings for Singles Held at Christ Church But Not Part of the Program

"Solo Flight"

Leader: Kay Collier-Slone

An ongoing divorce recovery support group which meets every Wednesday evening from 8:00 to 10:00 P.M. Suggested donation: $15.00 per meeting. Average attendance: four to five. Maximum attendance: nine. Members represent Episcopal, Presbyterian, Baptist, Roman Catholic. Non-Episcopal members frequently attend healing services and other services.

*   *   *   *   *

Projected Offerings Related to Singles' Ministry

"My Family Is Divorcing"

Leader: Kay Collier-Slone

Three separate six-week classes for six- to twelve-year-olds, teenagers, and adult children of divorce. This program is open to the diocese and community. It is hoped that donations will help defray the expenses involved in materials, etc.

"Solo Flight II"

Leader: Kay Collier-Slone

A biweekly/monthly (still not decided) Divorce Recovery Support Group for those who have healed the initial wounds but face ongoing—indeed life-long—issues involving repeated legal battles, remarriage, and ensuing problems, etc. This group has been requested by several individuals who have found themselves in dire need of support, and without understanding within most of their systems—from the family system, through the church system, to larger systems in society. Projected donation as in "Solo Flight."

*   *   *   *   *

IF *YOU*

WERE TO LOSE YOUR SPOUSE

TOMORROW . . .

OR IF YOU, YOUR SON, OR DAUGHTER

NEVER MARRIED . . .

AND YOU CAME TO CHRIST CHURCH

ALONE

WHAT WOULD YOU LOOK FOR?

WHERE WOULD YOU LOOK FOR IT?

WOULD YOU FIND IT?

* * *

"THE EPISCOPAL CHURCH WELCOMES YOU!"

the sign says . . .

Nearly 50% of the population is single today.
That statistic may be higher tomorrow.

WHAT DO OUR "SIGNS" SAY TO THAT SIZABLE

PORTION OF THE POPULATION

IN THIS DECADE OF EVANGELISM?

Why are these needs not being addressed?

1. We have a staff—clerical and lay—already focusing upon many
   diverse and important program areas; a staff aware of and sympa-
   thetic to the problem; a staff perhaps open to necessary funding or
   other assistance.

2. There is a general lack of awareness in society at large, and in the
   church in particular, as to the prevalence of the problem areas which
   have been mentioned, and other related areas, and to the ongoing
   nature of the problems.

3. There is a general reluctance in society to recognize the paradigm
   shift that has already happened. We are no longer predominantly a
   society of nuclear families. There are many nontraditional family
   and individual units that are with us—and with us to stay. Yet
   churches, like society, are geared to and comfortable with the old
   norms—coupled for life, or waiting to be, traditional family units.
   The multiple societal trends of transiency and upward mobility,
   young adults with greater freedom and flexibility marrying at a later
   age than in the past, and divorce as a widely accepted part of our
   society mean that there are greater numbers of people in every age
   group, every level of society devoid of traditional support systems of
   stable families, neighborhoods, communities.

4. There are fears that if we recognize "it," talk about "it," and make
   "it" a priority, the problem will become bigger, not better. A belief
   that the church must provide the model for marriage and family and
   traditional values. It has been said by several bishops, including our
   own, that such fears are among the major causes of the lack of recognition of these issues within the church. To recognize divorce
   and singleness, grief and change, is to acknowledge that they could,
   indeed, happen to us. That the pain of some of these issues are for
   many realities of life with which they must deal forever. That the
   further from the expected pattern of life "it" is—whatever the issue
   —the less chance that society, and the church, deal with "it"; minister to "it."

Brothers and Sisters in Christ . . .

This wonderful, dear church of ours has an opportunity to add to its already considerable ministry.

To be a leader, a true pioneer, in an area of ministry which needs leadership—which needs the considerable courage and vision it takes to be a pioneer.

I ask that as you conclude your reading of this information, we all make discernment of God's will in this area a special intention of our prayers.

Thank you for your time.

Faithfully,

Kay Collier-Slone
Spring, 1991

Resolution to Be Presented to Diocesan Convention regarding Single People within the Church
(Episcopal Diocese of Lexington, Kentucky, November, 1990)

WHEREAS, it is recognized that there are many single people in the church today who, collectively, constitute a unique and diverse group of Christians; and

WHEREAS, it is recognized that single people have unique spiritual needs as Christians; and

WHEREAS, it is the intention of the convention that the unique spiritual needs of single people be recognized and that each parish church in the diocese support and lift up the spirituality of single people.

NOW THEREFORE BE IT RESOLVED that the convention directs the clergy and laity of each parish church in the diocese to endeavor, with all deliberate speed, through programs, support groups, and other means, to draw single people in each parish into the life of the church; and

BE IT FURTHER RESOLVED that a standing committee of the diocese be established with the title "Commission on Singles Within the Church," and that such standing commission have the responsibilities of (1) conducting a study of the numbers, characteristics, and needs of single people within the church; and (2) providing guidance, support, and training programs to the parish churches in the diocese for the spiritual development of single people in the church; and

BE IT FURTHER RESOLVED that the study of the standing committee be completed within 180 days of the date that the standing committee is constituted by the bishop and that the committee's report, upon acceptance by the bishop, be published to all the parish churches of its diocese; and

BE IT FINALLY RESOLVED that the standing committee report at the next Diocesan Convention on the progress of the diocese and the parish churches in lifting up the spirituality of single people in the church.

The following article is reprinted from The Voice, *newspaper of the Diocese of Newark, New Jersey, April 1991.*

Singles Are Part of the Congregational Family, Too

by Kay Collier-Slone

A young woman of twenty-nine was in counseling. A life-long Episcopalian with a good job and growing savings account, she had broken off a long-term relationship. "I don't see many examples of good marriages," she said matter-of-factly towards the end of one session. "I really think that I'm going to buy my own home, find a sperm donor, and get on with my life."

A reality of the 1990s is that single is an option for many adults, no matter how they arrived at their singleness. In fact, roughly half of the adult population in the U.S. above the age of twenty-five is single. The common assumption that singleness is a transitional or temporary condition, an assumption generally held by those who are safely coupled and familied in the traditional sense, is being challenged.

"I have had several opportunities to remarry," said one attractive woman I know in her early fifties, divorced for eleven years. "Frankly, unless someone comes along to offer me something dramatically better than my present life, in terms of healthy companionship and shared values, that is not a choice I want to consider for my life—and I underscore the word choice!"

And a single man told me once, "In my singleness I have some nice options and freedoms. A part of me believes, however, that my sometime-sadness has to do with believing that we were created to live in relationship, and that given the right option, I could be even happier than I am now, but I won't just marry anyone in order not to be single."

But the world at large is not attuned to singleness as an option—as a state equal to, not lesser than, that of being coupled. And neither is a church which so often identifies itself in family terms.

A recent check of the Yellow Pages for three different cities with populations over 300,000 revealed a maximum of four churches advertising singles' ministries, while many listed such attractions as family services, nursery care or youth programs.

Most often singles' ministry is considered a part of crisis ministry—ministry to people grief-stricken over the loss of a spouse through death or to people feeling failed and rejected because of a divorce.

But what about the widowed or divorced who begin to experience the subtle turning-away of long-time coupled friends or the fact that activities which once included them no longer do?

"I didn't have any idea I would lose so many friends, too," said one young widow, now parenting two small children alone. "They just don't include me anymore."

Where there is an effort to organize singles' ministries the attitude too often is that the purpose is only that of dating and mating. An elderly widower called recently to inquire about a singles' conference. He was, he stressed, quite good at taking care of himself, but he was lonely, and looking for companionship with others who wanted compatible intellectual and spiritual friends of both sexes, hastening to add, "I'm not going to tell you my name, because I don't want you to think I'm a dirty old man."

Singles' ministries in Episcopal churches most typically arise when a small group of singles in a parish decide to do something for themselves. Ages and interests shape the activities until the volunteer leaders run out of energy. The group fades away or finds its way to another organization in the community.

Any group dependent on personal neediness and devoid of institutional support and recognition is doomed to suffer the same fate.

The reality of the world of singleness is so incredibly broad and complex that it is little wonder that the church, like the rest of society, has not even begun to address the issue.

Where does one begin? Should it be addressed from an intergenerational perspective, or the interest-group perspective? Should it be a parish ministry, a multi-parish ministry or a diocesan ministry? Should it emphasize a pastoral approach, dealing with concerns arising from recovery issues, personal esteem issues, sexuality issues, or the sadness and isolation presented by the holidays, or should it emphasize a networking, social approach?

In Atlanta, ESP (Every Single Person) at Holy Innocents' Episcopal Church was begun three years ago as a parish program and an extended ministry to the community under the direction of Dr. John Stathas, a psychotherapist on the staff of the parish who was single more years of his adult life than he now has been married. He feels that those years definitely gave him a sensitivity to the needs and issues of the people with whom he ministers. A portion of his work is spent in counseling group members who are involved in new relationships, helping them to discern the health and appropriateness of the relationship.

"The factors that make this ministry go are institutional support, the fact that it is both an extended and outreach ministry that takes care of the special needs of singles in the parish, and the fact that it is holistic, involving their spiritual, intellectual, physical and emotional lives," Stathas said. "It has a high percentage of men due to the fact that we often meet in the lounge of an athletic club where the men feel comfortable and safe."

In Spartanburg, South Carolina, the Rev. Mike Lumpkin is rector of St. Christopher's Episcopal Church, a congregation in which an estimated thirty percent of the members are single, covering a wide range of categories. Specific programs have included one called K.I.D.S. (Kids in Divorce Situations). But more importantly, Lumpkin tries to insure that every activity in his parish is represented by singles. "I want single people among the vestry nominees, on new committees, among the readers at festival services like Lessons and Carols," he said. "I want this issue in the forefront of the minds of the leadership of the parish. When we have programs coming up I send a personal letter to the singles mailing list, asking them to participate."

Lumpkin, who himself spent many years as an adult single, believes that most single people, if not specifically asked, are less likely to volunteer. "They have very busy lives—some are single parents, with all that implies, and it's also harder for a single person to come to a church function by themselves," he said. "Those who say it isn't haven't tried it. You have to work at it—get up the gumption, bring a friend."

We are no longer predominantly a society of traditional, nuclear families. There are many non-traditional and individual family units already with us, and with us to stay. Yet there seems to be a fear that if we recognize this, and talk about it or make it a ministry priority, that the problem will become bigger, not better. But history has shown that when minority groups do not get heard, or their needs and concerns receive, at best, only token notice, they will eventually protest.

"I just don't understand," one single professional said to me recently. "I have a good job. I contribute generously to my church. I will never have a teenager to use the youth-group van, and while I don't mind giving to youth work and other ministries, if some of my pledge can't go toward a real singles ministry in this church, I'll find a church where it will."

When singles ministries function well, evangelism occurs. "It took me two years to get up the nerve to come to this church because everyone seemed to be attached to someone," one thirty-five-year-old professional man told me. "And it's only since there has been some effort at a singles group that I feel I have friends here who really accept me and appreciate me for who I am."

The challenge to the church is not only to live into and minister to today's world, but also to learn from it as we are propelled into the further challenges of a new century. For this new century will require that we prayerfully embrace our polymorphic constituency in ministry which actualizes our claim: "The Episcopal Church Welcomes You."

Program Planning Overview and Process

Saint Michael and All Angels Episcopal Church
Dallas, Texas
(Reprinted with permission.)

Questions for Discussion and Reflection:
Singles' Review 1990-1991

September 21-22, 1990

1. Whether it was three months or three years ago, try to think back to when you first became involved with the singles at St. Michael. What significant needs prompted you to get involved?

2. What is going on today that is most rewarding with the singles' ministry—programs, study, fellowship, friendship, a sense of family, divorce or single parents—whatever?

   Where do you feel frustrated about any of the areas above, about the singles' ministry at SMAA—or any other areas of concern you have?

3. How have your needs as a single person changed or evolved since you became involved with the singles' ministry at SMAA? What is happening and what is missing that corresponds with those needs?

4. What gifts and talents have you contributed to the singles' ministry here in the past? How would you see yourself involved in the present and in the future: i.e., what are your talents, abilities, and passions, and where do you want to channel them? What could you get excited about?

PROGRAM PLANNING OVERVIEW

PROGRAMS: CURRENT STRUCTURE	PROGRAMS: POTENTIAL IDEAS	PROGRAM PURPOSE	LEADERSHIP REQUIRED	AREA FOR CHANGE	DISCUSSION QUESTIONS
What events are you currently sponsoring?	What events would you like to sponsor?	What area of identified need is the event addressing?	How many leaders are needed? What are their roles? Is a committee necessary?	Does this item require revision?	1. What is meant by: "The responsibility for a program that rests on one person will eventually die"? 2. What does it take to start building "big people" rather than "big programs"? 3. Why is change necessary for a healthy ministry?

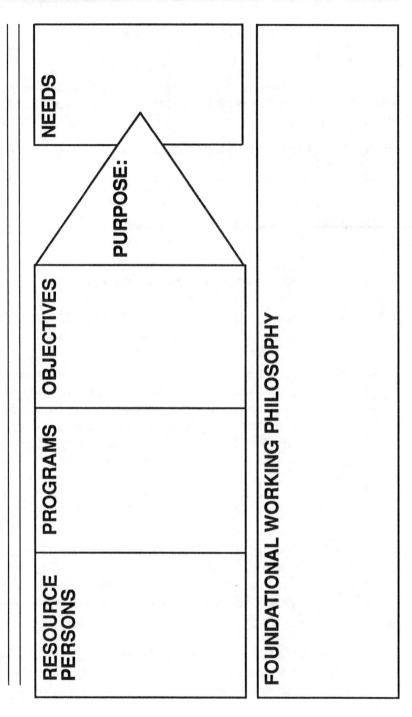

Program Planning Overview

With a strong foundation, effective programming can become reality. Without it, the results are destined to be frustrating, superficial, short-lived, or built only on hype.

Here is a seven-step process to help in building a foundation, or reevaluating an existing one.

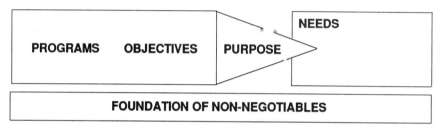

| PROGRAMS | OBJECTIVES | PURPOSE | NEEDS |

FOUNDATION OF NON-NEGOTIABLES

STEP ONE: Pray for insight, intuition, wisdom, sensitivity, and other stuff that will help you maintain a clear focus.

STEP TWO: Affirm our foundational principles. In which direction are we headed? What spiritual principles are we building our ministry upon? What are the distinguishing characteristics of our programming emphasis? What are the foundational principles of our church and how *does* our planning and programming reflect them. Will we try to break down stereotypes? Which ones? Will we look at people not just programs? How? Is "service" our focus?

STEP THREE: Identify needs. What are we aiming at? Who are we focusing on? Brainstorm together. Picture the people to whom we minister. Who do you see? Picture their faces, their circumstances, their needs. What do you see that makes you sad? Angry? Encouraged?

*NOTE: When Christ saw peoples' needs, they evoked intense emotions in Him. He cried, felt compassion, was sad, and threw people out of the temple. Jesus knew what was at stake. Look with the eyes of you heart to see where people are incomplete, where they hurt, where they face life alone and afraid. On the arrow, list areas of need that come to mind. Attempt to distinguish between felt and unfelt needs. (A felt need would be the anger and pain from the ending of a relationship; the unfelt need would be the healing process, perhaps in the context of a small group.)

STEP FOUR: Creating a purpose statement. The needs will determine the specific focus of our ministry and thus our programming. The purpose statement is a general statement that sets the tone for the ministry. Write three or four sample purpose statements, one to three sentences in length, no more. Begin the sample statements with, "In response to the needs we see, our purpose is . . ." or "We exist . . ."

STEP FIVE: Objectives. Objectives are broad, non-measurable categories or areas of focus. They indicate the involvement necessary to fulfill the purpose. Example:

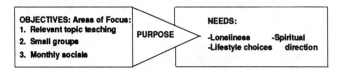

STEP SIX: Programs. Based on identification of needs, purpose, and objectives, what specific programs do we need? Example:

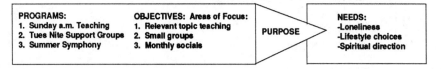

STEP SEVEN: Discuss any obstacles to achieving your purpose.

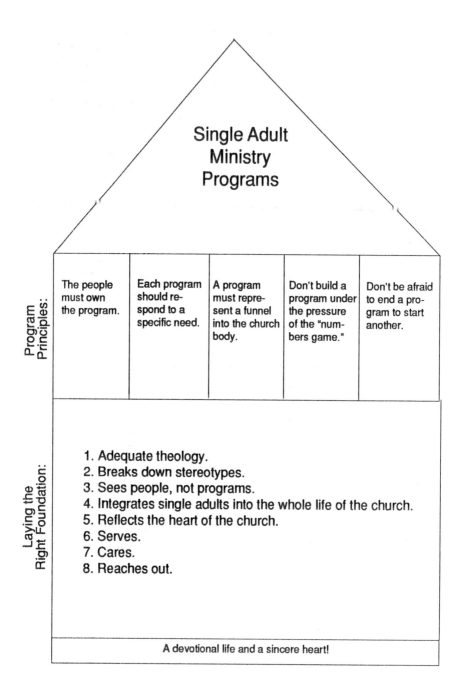

Single Adult Ministry Programs

Program Principles:

| The people must own the program. | Each program should respond to a specific need. | A program must represent a funnel into the church body. | Don't build a program under the pressure of the "numbers game." | Don't be afraid to end a program to start another. |

Laying the Right Foundation:

1. Adequate theology.
2. Breaks down stereotypes.
3. Sees people, not programs.
4. Integrates single adults into the whole life of the church.
5. Reflects the heart of the church.
6. Serves.
7. Cares.
8. Reaches out.

A devotional life and a sincere heart!

Leadership Covenant: Single Adult Ministry

Jesus told them, "In this world the kings and great men order their slaves around, and the slaves have no choice but to like it! But among you, the one who serves you best will be your leader. Out in the world the master sits at the table and is served by his servants. But not here! For I am your servant."

Luke 22:25-26 (TLB)

In signing this covenant, I am agreeing to serve with

_____

for a period of _____ months,
beginning _____ and ending _____ .
I understand that I become part of a community of leaders with whom I
pursue personal and corporate growth, peace,
healing, and love within the community.

_____

Signature

Activities Planning Survey

To help us plan future activities, please circle any of the following events you would attend. Also, we are looking for people to be a chairperson for each event and be responsible for organizing it and therefore be able to attend it free. If that interests you, and you have the ability to plan and organize one of these events, please let us know at the bottom of this form.

Sports
1. volleyball
2. softball
3. raquetball
4. tennis
5. biking
6. basketball
7. football
8. baseball
9. hockey
10. roller skating
11. water skiing
12. fishing
13. snow skiing
14. golf tourney
15. bowling league
16. hiking
17. _____

Theater and the Arts
18. dinner playhouse
19 first-run movies
20. plays
21. musicals
22. art museums
23. church choir
24. art classes
25. photography club
26. other _____

Travel
27. train to _____
28. bus to _____
29. carpool to _____
30. observatories
31. amusement parks
32. other _____

Seminary Topics
33. tax planning
34. nutritional health
35. know what we believe
36. personal finance
37. relational skills
38. assertiveness training
39. sexuality
40. divorce-recovery workshop
41. parent effectiveness
42. small group leader
43. intimacy
44. self-esteem
45. stress management
46. personal appearance
47. job search skills
48. other

_____

_____

_____

YES! I'm interested in being a chairperson for this/there event(s),
leading the organization and planning and involving others as necessary.

1. _____   2. _____
3. _____   4. _____

Name _____
Address _____

_____

Telephone _____ (H)

_____ (W)

Team Report

Name _____

Area _____

Date _____

1. I need decisions from you for the following items:

2. I am having a problem with the following:

3. I am planning to:

4. I am making progress in the following areas:

5. I would like to rate my personal happiness factor at: _____
   (1 = suicidal; 100 = best I've ever been). I say this because:

6. Please pray for me in the following areas:

Principles of Team Membership

Always be willing to do more than your share.

Everyone works less hard.

Never say uncomplimentary things about another team member behind his or her back.

Not only is this "gutless" behavior, it destroys team communications.

Confront your conflicts.

It is emotionally less expensive; resolved conflicts strengthen relationships.

Never be late or absent for trivial reasons.

To do so is unfair to your teammates who must carry your load.

Be involved, concerned, and active in your own personal growth.

Team development and personal growth cannot be separated.

Contribute to the personal growth of other team members whenever it is appropriate.

The results will be a stronger you and a stronger team.

Participate in team activities even when it is inconvenient to do so.

Participation facilitates self-disclosure and mutual respect which are important to team development.

Accept reality. All members do not have the same duties, experience, and ability.

What Do the Individuals on Staff Do?

Your staff person will be of great help and support to you if you let him or her be. Remember, we are working together as a team, so it is important to the ministry that you stay in touch and work together.

Responsibilities of Staff:

TO encourage you in your ministry. It is not the responsibility of staff to do your ministry. By encouragement, we mean help to accomplish your goals and to make sure you have the resources you need.

TO remind you to incorporate others into your area of ministry. It is not staff's responsibility to get people for you. You will develop a list of people who want to be involved in your area of ministry and it is your responsibility to follow them up.

TO communicate with you about what is happening in the overall ministry. Good communication is important so you can see the bigger picture; when we see the bigger picture, we can work better as a team.

TO help you work through your difficulties and frustrations in your ministry. Staff does not necessarily have the answers, but sometimes it helps to know they care and will listen. They are to serve you when it gets tough. They can't do your job, but they can come alongside you and support you.

TO be a part of seeing your dreams come true. Share your ideas with them and allow them to help decide whether or not they are feasible. You may have great ideas which the ministry is not quite ready for.

TO approve you plans and to make sure you are being financially responsible.

TO make sure you get approval for events. If you want to be provided with finances for your ministry, you must go through the proper channels.

How Can You Help the Staff Do Their Ministry?

The ministry staff is like the coaching staff of a sports team. They rally the team and motivate it toward a common goal. They are chosen to help you be successful, to win, and they do best when you help them to win also. The way you best help the staff is to be a team player; there is no place in ministry for lone rangers.

Procedures

There are times when some common consideration will help the team to perform at its best:

1. When you can't make a leadership team meeting, please contact the facilitators of your team or your committee heads and let them know you can't make it.

2. If you do have to miss a meeting, throw yourself at the mercy of the team! Beg forgiveness and promise never to miss another meeting. It is your responsibility to find out what happened in your absence and what decisions were made. When you miss a meeting, your absence indicates your automatic approval of all suggestions.

3. Make sure dates for all events are phoned into the office. It is very important that the office knows all planned events, even small leadership meetings or outings.

4. Every leader is responsible for all monies requested and spent in their areas. There are procedures to follow to request money and all funds must be properly accounted for at the end of each event. If the procedures are not complied with, you must do the following: (1) cash in your savings account and pay back the unreported funds, (2) repent, and (3) pledge your first-born (or first-adopted) child.

5. Each leader is asked to turn in a monthly report form. If you don't have

a blank form, too bad ... that's not a good enough reason! Get some new forms and turn one in.

6. You are asked to meet at least monthly with the leadership of your ministry area(s) to encourage them and make sure they are supported.

7. It is your responsibility to recruit new leaders for the area of ministry you are overseeing. The person you choose as leader should be agreed upon by the rest of the leadership team and staff.

8. If you see a problem person in the ministry, discuss what to do at your next leadership meeting. It is important to alert staff to the problem.

9. If you have a complaint, write it down and put it in an envelope. Put the envelope in your clothes dresser. In a week or two, pull it out and see if the issue is still a problem of major importance.

The DISCOVERY Program

A Plan for Ministry of, to, and by Single Persons
for St. Michael and All Angels Church
January 13, 1987
(Reprinted with permission.)

Written by the Rev. Thomas Blackmon for The Singles' Planning Committee: Mr. Mark D. Blake, Ms. Karen Cornett, Mr. Jim Harell, Mr. Jim Henry, Ms. Helen Long, Ms. Elaine Mizell, Ms. Karen Nelson, Ms. Jo Phillips, Ms. Ann Ross, Mr. Mike Shanley, Ms. Kathryn Steininger, and Mr. Tom Toland

Beginning with Theology

Early in his ministry, an incident occurred that is very illuminating for all of us disciples who are trying to follow our Lord's call to be disciples for the gospel in today's world. Caught late in the afternoon at an isolated place with a crowd of hungry people, the disciples come to Jesus and ask him to send the crowd away to buy their own food. Jesus responds simply and directly: "You give them something to eat." The message in that response seems clear to me—as our Lord has fed us, so are we called to feed others. Ministry to other people makes sense because you and I know what it means to be in need of a shepherd ourselves and to have felt our Lord's compassionate response to our need. Continuing this work of reconciliation begun in Christ is the warrant for all ministry and the measure against which all ministry must be evaluated.

With the theological foundation in mind, what do we see as we survey the culture around us? I believe one painful reality we see everywhere is that of refugees. The dictionary defines refugees as people "who are homeless, rootless, hungry, not speaking the language of other people." The world these days is full of refugees—from Southern Asia and Africa, Central America, the Soviet Union. Many are feeling political turmoil while others seek some kind of economic stability. But there is another large group of refugees who have not come by boat, over mountains, or across rivers—they are already among us on every side. The people I have in mind are single people in America—our "relational" refugees. They do not know where they fit in this country that still sees itself as a nation of "nuclear families." There are now some eighty million of them in America, over half under the age of thirty-five. Many are single out of necessity (divorce and widowhood), but many others out of choice. They have particular needs and they offer some special gifts, each coming from their particular life experiences as single persons. Both our scripture and tradition remind us of the special role refugees have played in the working out of God's plans for this world—from Adam and Eve, and Abraham and Sarah, right down to the present day. The challenge for us is to reach out to them in caring for those needs, and, at the same time, to call forth their gifts for the work of all God's people in this place.

Who Are They and Where Are They?

The single population is, quite literally, all around us. Nationally, almost forty-eight percent of all adults are single, reflecting steadily increasing numbers since 1960. The median age for first marriages has increased 2.5 years since 1970, and the national divorce rate stands right at thirty-five percent (here in Dallas County, it is fifty percent). It is these kinds of statistics which make it clear how rapidly the single population in America is increasing and will continue to climb. The trends are clear. Closer to home—in the ten zip codes in which most of our parishioners live—the population is forty-seven percent single, of whom sixty percent have never been married.[1] These percentages match almost perfectly those for our own parish. Of our 4,000 plus communicants, 2,100 are single and between the ages of twenty-two and seventy-five. This includes at least 243 single parents.[2] They thus constitute 52.5 percent of our communicant strength and already contribute to our parish life in many ways—singing in the choir, volunteering in the Church School and

---

1. The zip codes are: 48, 40, 34, 29, 25, 30, 20, 09, 05, and 06. Source: Donnelly Demographics.
2. These data from our computer records *exclude* over 1,000 people for whom we have no birthdate at all.

Youth Ministry, working on the Altar Guild and as ushers, and so much more. Of course, they do not make these contributions as "single people"; so they are, in a sense, invisible, but they would surely have an impact were they absent. In 1985, they also contributed $374,313 to the operating budget of our parish. In our ten neighborhood zip codes, they are relatively affluent (average income is $24,000 compared to $16,500 for Dallas County) and well educated (14.5 years education on the average compared to 12.5 years for Dallas County as a whole). To para-phrase the immortal Pogo "we have met the singles, and they are us." What is disturbing, however, is how many single people are unchurched, especially those under age thirty-five and those who are divorced. Statistics gathered by The Alban Institute estimate these numbers at between fifty-five and sixty-five percent. Therein lies both a judgment on churches—who often behave as if this reality is an illusion or irrelevant—and an opportunity for churches who are caring, creative, and secure enough to move out and meet these people where they are. Moving out and meeting at St. Michael is what this plan for ministry is about.

Where Did This Plan Come From?

When Bob Ratelle called me to join his staff in May of 1984, he charged me with helping to develop the most comprehensive approach possible for working with single people. Initially, model programs were developed with two groups of singles among whom I saw the most pressing need—younger singles and single parents. Building on what has been learned from that work during the past eighteen months, the time has come to make a quantum jump in our ministry program. Awareness, energy, and expectations have all been raised and the time is right. In June, therefore, I convened a diverse group of single people to join me in developing this plan. Their names are listed on the front page of this report. Some have been at St. Michael and All Angels forever, others for just a few years. They vary greatly as to age, occupation, marital history, and program priorities, but they all came to the project with a shared commitment and a willingness to work. They have been a pleasure to work with. Since June, each of them has spent some thirty hours in meetings and more hours doing research and other "homework" I asked them to do. They have worked together with grace and intensity.

This is as much their report as mine, and I am proud of them and very thankful to them all for their ministries in giving this report life and shape.

Mission Statement for the DISCOVERY Ministry

We began our work together by discussing what single people need from our church and what they have to offer. Soon we found ourselves pushing toward a "purpose statement," and this is the result. This statement was developed through many drafts from the beginning of the planning process right through to its completion. Thus, it reflects what we learned as we went along and some significant changes were made. It is guided by our theological self understanding, and that theological self understanding includes these four affirmations:

1. We all need God.
2. We all need each other.
3. God is revealed to us as we live in community and serve one another.
4. As we live and serve, we all have much to learn about giving and receiving.

Ministry of, by, and to single people at St. Michael is therefore intended to:

1. Affirm and enrich our lives as spiritual persons through opportunities for worship, learning, service, recreation, and mutual support.
2. Create and nurture opportunities for growth and relaxation that are healthy, honest, and respectful of our diversity (that is, as to gender, marital history, economic status, etc.).
3. Encourage an atmosphere of belonging and acceptance that acknowledges us as single persons, and, at the same time, enables us to be integrated more fully into the life of the parish as a whole.
4. Open up new avenues for sharing the special gifts that single people consistently bring to church life—innovativeness, enthusiasm, staying power, flexibility, creative use of our time.

What Single People at St. Michael Say They Want

This is just a short version of the long "shopping list" of wants and needs that our planning committee gathered through interviewing and surveying many single people here at St. Michael.

1. A warm, comfortable physical space to gather in for fellowship and study.

2. A church community that can be a "balancing place" helping us to be more whole persons in terms of our spiritual, emotional, intellectual, and physical being.

3. Practicing and living out models for healthy Christian relationships both romantic and platonic.

4. A caring community of mutual support and acceptance to counter feelings of isolation and loneliness.

5. Programs that offer time and space to relax and laugh so essential to building closeness between people.

6. Various resources for counseling in the midst of acute personal crises such as separation and divorce.

7. Information and training for life (from how to deal with sexually transmitted diseases to financial planning to career development to personal spiritual growth).

8. Spiritual and theological programs to focus on the centrality of our sacramental worship life and enable us to be better informed and more secure as Christians.

9. Opportunities for developing enhanced self-acceptance as a single person in a society which still understands itself essentially in terms of adult couples.

10. Several church school opportunities on Sunday mornings targeted at single people.

What Is Happening for Single Persons in Other Nearby Churches?

After gathering information from single people within our parish, the planning committee then developed a two-page survey to use in other parishes—episcopalians and non-episcopalians—here in north Dallas. Each member of the planning committee was assigned to several churches and asked to make an appointment with one or more of the singles' ministers in each of these churches. Interviews conducted averaged two hours in length and the data were gathered, collated, and shared. We discovered, not to our surprise, that very little is going on for single persons in any organized way in any other episcopal church in the Diocese of Dallas. There is one singles' group at Incarnation and a very small and fragile one at Transfiguration. We were also able to reaffirm what we already knew—that the methodists, baptists, and presbyterians have, as usual, stolen about a five-year march on episcopalians when it comes to responding to a special area of programming need. The churches we surveyed included First Methodist and First Presbyterian downtown, Highland Park Memorial, Highland Park Presbyterian, Lovers Lane Methodist, the Jewish Community Center, and Park Cities Baptist Church. In brief, these are some of the patterns we found:

1. More women are involved than men.
2. There is little funding support in most places.
3. There are a lot of social activities.
4. There is a strong desire to be part of a larger family.
5. There is a strong desire to grow spiritually.
6. There is an emphasis on interpersonal relations in educational programs.
7. Groups are divided by age and interest.

We also discovered some clear prerequisites for a successful and productive ministry to single people in all of the churches we surveyed. These key common factors are:

1. Sunday morning classes for single persons.
2. Publicity that is frequent, well done, upbeat, and personal.
3. An adequate budget.

4. Some full-time professional staff.
5. An umbrella group or "singles' council" to help coordinate programs, planning, and evaluation.
6. A high-energy nucleus of lay people who share leadership, take real responsibility and have decision-making power.
7. A mixture of activities that balances social, service, and learning.
8. Presence of a counseling center in the church helps a great deal.
9. Special support groups for newly divorced persons, single parents, the unemployed, gay persons, and others under special stress.

Some negative things that we noticed invariably included:

1. Where there is too much emphasis on the social, the group begins to disintegrate.
2. Where there is a lack of space and facilities, groups tend to disintegrate.
3. Where there is a lack of care and knowledge of the problems that single people particularly face, there is often a stereotyping of single people that drives them away.
4. A lack of commitment to stay with programs on the part of single people themselves.
5. Because these efforts are so new, there is a lack of clear models on what kind of ministry programs are successful.
6. The universal withdrawal of many men from church life when they divorce.
7. Where there is no budget and staff support, the ministry often fails to get off the ground or remains small in numbers, diversity, and scope.

A final thing that we noticed about a number of other church programs for single persons is that they deliberately separated this ministry from the rest of the parish. Oftentimes, singles' groups worship, learn, serve, and play completely apart from the remainder of the parish. As episcopalians, all of us on the planning committee and every other single person in our parish surveyed agreed that this is not a pattern we want here in the community. On the contrary, we aim to help single people feel more whole as persons and thus to feel more integrated in the life of this parish as a whole. We came to some conclusions out of all of this survey material which are as follows:

Our Conclusions

1. We will not try to create a lot of small, specialized congregations within the body.
2. It is essential to keep our liturgical focus central and to keep our worship from becoming personality centered.
3. It is essential to maintain a balance between learning, worship, service, and social activities.
4. It is essential to maintain a "non-hustling" atmosphere of acceptance and cooperation. This has been done among the younger singles and single parents.
5. Well written, clear, and abundant publicity material is absolutely critical.
6. Both professional and volunteer leadership must be energetic, committed, imaginative, and entrepreneurial.
7. A warm, versatile physical space to call "home" is a big plus.
8. A healthy balance is needed between financial support frm the parish and financial support from participants.

Using the generalizations that emerged from all of our interviewing and surveys, the planning committee brainstormed some program principles. We believe that we must always keep these principles in front of us as we develop specific activities and events to serve people, because they are the norms we need to evaluate programs in an ongoing way. The principles we identified are:

Our Program Principles

1. Each program or activity should respond to a specific need, either stated or felt.
2. Programs should represent a funnel, directly or indirectly, into the

larger body of the parish (programs that help single persons build their sense of self-esteem and their sense of belonging will do this indirectly. Single people helping out in various church programs or events may contribute to this more directly).

3. Single people themselves must own the programs. It cannot be handed down on high from a priest or other professional staff. In other words, when we look at the ministry, we need to see people first and programs second. The programs should be built around lay leadership and clergy support and guidance.

4. We cannot build a program that is authentic under the pressure of the numbers game. This does not mean that numbers are unimportant, but an anecdote may be instructive; Lovers Lane began its singles' ministry program seventeen years ago with fifty or sixty people involved. At the end of three years, between 150 and 200 were significantly involved and only after this period of building did that ministry explode into what it has become today. Already here at St. Michael, our programs for single people touch eighty persons/week.

5. The "guru" mentality should be vigorously avoided. Lay leadership should be diverse and dynamic, mixing continuity and change. Clergy and other professional leadership should be empowering, not egocentric.

6. We must never be afraid to stop a program or activity that has outlived its usefulness and begin doing something new that is more effective. This means ongoing evaluation.

What Ministry Objectives Have We Identified?

With these principles and our data in mind, we next identified general objectives and prioritized them in the following order:

1. Offer a balanced ministry to single persons which will enable and encourage them to grow spiritually and in their relationship with Christ.

2. Put into place a professional singles' ministry staff, including adequate support staff and energetic, creative ordained leadership.

3. Achieve an enhanced level of individual commitment and group

involvement of single people across the board at St. Michael.

4. Maintain a healthy balance in programs and activities between community, recreational, psychological, and theological concerns.
5. Experiment with and assess ministry models which might be used in other churches as well as at St. Michael, maintaining flexibility and openness as the touchstones for success.
6. Produce a variety of different publicity materials to share information and concerns among single people.
7. Successfully raise the awareness of the whole parish about who and where single people are, what their concerns are, and what their gifts are in order to break down the kind of stereotyping about singles that has occurred in the past in this parish.
8. Remedy the under-utilization of the talents of our single people, and build the kind of leadership that uses the gifts of many and will enable us both to serve others and keep our own leadership dynamic.
9. Maintain a ministry that does not allow an excessive focus on self, but attends to the key Gospel truth that one saves one's life by losing it.
10. Offer programs that take into account the reality that self-acceptance and healthy relationships are critical spiritual and social issues for single people.
11. Offer specific programs for single people in the midst of traumatic transitions.
12. Fully utilize the potential for learning and group building offered by the Sunday morning educational hour.
13. Have a warm, comfortable, efficient place for single people to work and play, and have up-to-date equipment to use for both.

Based on these general objectives, we established some specific goals for 1987:

1987 Goals

1. Establish an umbrella Singles' Council in the second quarter of 1987 to guide (policy), coordinate (networking), and plan and evaluate (research)—to consist of persons of varying ages, interests, skills, and marital history.

2. Locate and employ a Singles' Activity Coordinator whose responsibilities would be administration, financial control, and publicity. It is anticipated that this would be a half-time job in the second half of 1987.

3. Develop newsletters on a monthly basis for each of our singles' groups and supplement these newsletters with regular publicity (fliers announcing specific events and programs), by April 1, 1987 (two monthly newsletters already in place).

4. Expand the Tuesday night format already being used by the Younger Singles (fellowship/supper/program/worship) to every Tuesday for differing singles' groups: one for Younger Singles, one for Middle Singles, and one for more Mature Singles, so that each Tuesday night is a "Singles' Evening" at St. Michael. On a quarterly basis these Tuesday evenings would gather all of the singles' groups into a major supper/speaker evening, to begin January, 1987.

5. Initiate a group for the "suddenly single"—persons going through an acutely painful time of separation or divorce. This group should be organized along the lines of a workshop and take place two or three times a year, for six weeks at a time, to begin January, 1987.

6. Develop a useable, easily accessible, and adequate information system for single people at St. Michael that will enable us to know what we need to know about them and communicate with them about events, birthdays, etc., by autumn, 1987.

7. Complete the refurbishing of 4406 Colgate for use by Youth Ministry and by DISCOVERY by April 1, 1987.

8. Establish a Stewardship group within the Singles' Council to begin work on stewardship of time, talent, and treasure among single people at St. Michael. This will involve a survey in detail of the talents and activity interests of single people, to be initiated by autumn of 1987.

9. Using the model for retreats developed with the Younger Singles, initiate a more extensive retreat program for a variety of single persons, to begin by autumn of 1987.

10. Provide leadership training for volunteer leaders within the various singles' groups to focus on small group leadership, motivation, organizational skills, planning, scripture study, etc.

11. Initiate small group Bible study and other discussion groups for single people of all ages that focus on the relation of faith to everyday living, using models developed for Younger Singles.

12. Maintain and deepen the burgeoning Younger Singles' Ministry already in place at St. Michael, building on the strong sense of community and mutual support present, and making special efforts to capitalize on that community for increased service to church and community.
13. Provide impetus for a national examination of ministry to single persons around the whole Episcopal Church with a view toward building friendships, sharing and learning, and influencing the ministry program to be presented by the church's Executive Council at the 1988 General Convention.

Budget Needs for 1987

Communication and Publicity

$2,700.00	* Monthly newsletters for Younger, Middle, and Mature Singles' groups (2,500 copies per month x twelve months x three groups = 90,000 copies)
300.00	* Occasional notices for the Single Parents, Suddenly Separate, and other "special interest" groups (total of 10,000 copies)
350.00	* Two-color general information brochure on the DISCOVERY ministry (2,000 copies)
750.00	* Singles hot-line
360.00	* Special two-color fliers and posters for "supper" speakers and events scheduled for January 30-31, March 28-29, October 9-10, and November 14-15 (100 posters, 400 fliers)
1,200.00	* Postage and duplicating
$5,660.00	Total (divided by 12 = $471.66/month)

Leadership Development and Networking

$ 100.00	* Membership in National Association of Single Adults (N.A.S.A.)

1,000.00	* Training in developing "covenant," Bible study, and other small learning groups
1,000.00	* Organizational development training: planning, finance, collaborative management, evaluation
2,300.00	* Network development and resource sharing, both ecumenical and among episcopalians
2,000.00	* Partial support for attendance of leadership teams to N.A.S.A. national conference in Kansas City in September, 1987 and Episcopal Singles' Network in December, 1987
<u>120.00</u>	* Subscriptions to publications
$6,520.00	Total

Learning Programs

$1,500.00	* Twenty Sunday morning programs for the Younger Singles' class (which meets 46 Sundays/year)
400.00	* Quarterly evening programs for all single people
-0-	* Quarterly weekend retreats (led by ATB)
3,000.00	* Special programs for all single people, as well as other interested parishioners

$2,200.00	1. In January, the Rev. Terry Hershey on "Intimacy" (with College Ministry)
2,000.00	2. In March, the Rev. John Westerhoff/ Caroline Hughes on "Conflict" (with C.E.)
400.00	3. In May, the Rev. Darrell Hallbick on "Relationships"
1,800.00	4. In October, the Rev. John Bradshaw on "Creativity and Communication"
1,000.00	5. In November, Dr. Verna Dozier, Bible study retreat
(4,400.00)	6. Income derived from fees for the above special programs

450.00   * Divorce recovery workshops (winter, summer, fall)
<u>800.00</u>   * Partial scholarships for retreats and special programs.

$6,150.00   Total

Personnel

$15,000.00   * A part-time position of Activities Coordinator
               (perhaps to be shared with the business office).
               Package includes salary, FICA, and benefits for
               twenty four hours/week. ($15,000.00 divided by
               fifty-two weeks = $288.00/week, or about
               $1,150.00/month.)
<u>10,000.00</u>   * A part-time position of teacher/counselor. A
               woman is probably desirable.

$25,000.00   Total

Information Systems Equipment

The limitations of our current church computer system works a real
hardship on any church program where communication of activities,
people mobility and turnover, evangelism and growth, building stewardship, etc., are critical factors. Nowhere is this more true than in working
with single people. Thus, some new hardware and software is required.
Knowledgeable single people have investigated and recommended the
following purchases:

$1,200.00   * Panasonic "Senior Partner" or Corona PPC400
               machine.
307.00   * "Farsight," "pfs:WRITE," and "pfs:File" software.
<u>690.00</u>   * "PICK" system database package.

$2,197.00   Total

$45,527.00   Grand total

In 1988, we would strive to maintain the work expanded in 1987 while
adding these new pieces to the ministry:

Additional 1988 Goals

1. Design and initiate at least one "covenant group" for each of the age-range singles' groups and one across age lines for persons especially interested in establishing a close and small mutual support group and more focused spiritual rule of life. These might include elements found in groups such as those established by the Cross of Nails network of Coventry Cathedral. The design phase would be preceded by a research phase (looking for models) and the responsibility for this would rest on a committee generated out of the Singles' Council. Groups would be launched in September, 1988.

2. Develop co-educational and/or separate men's and/or women's sports activities that are open to all in softball, volleyball, basketball, etc. This would also be a spin-off from the Singles' Council and begin with the spring of 1988 softball season.

3. Develop out of the Singles' Council an Evangelism Committee that would devise and implement an "episcopalian" approach to evangelizing unchurched single people, particularly in such densely single areas as "The Village." This evangelism effort would begin its major outreach in June of 1988.

4. Locate and furnish a full-time "place" for single persons at St. Michael to gather, study, break bread, plan and play, including kitchen facilities and multi-use meeting space. To be used by all single folks, it would hopefully become a magnet for St. Michael's parishioners and for newcomers as well. By June 1, 1988.

5. Develop cohesive singles' Bible study groups for all ages using the Verna Dozier and Kerygma approaches to Bible study. Lay leadership would need to be recruited and trained in the first half of 1988 and the groups begun in September of 1988.

6. Organize and offer a variety of travel opportunities (perhaps one per quarter) for all single persons that involve recreation, learning, and service (at least once a year) and keep costs as reasonable as possible.

7. Expand leadership training opportunities for single persons using the Singles' Council to identify training needs, costs, and resources.

8. Move to promote in an intentional way the movement of single people into positions of responsibility and authority in the Men and Women of St. Michael, the Parish Council, the Vestry, etc.

9. Take on and fulfill a major service project in the greater Dallas area that would challenge many singles to share their gifts in a novel way and in a setting other than North Dallas. This would be accomplished through the Singles' Council and might or might not involve a joint venture with other parish outreach programs. To begin in summer of 1988. Initiated by the Singles' Council.

10. Take the initiative to establish an organized ministry to single persons at the diocesan level, using the experience and resources of this very large parish to assist and enable others.

11. Expand the Activities Coordinator and Teacher/Counselor positions into full-time jobs by January 1, 1988.

12. Undertake a comprehensive evaluation of the DISCOVERY program to date using the Singles' Council and consultant assistance. This would begin in January of 1988 and be complete by April 1.

13. Provide impetus for an organized "presence" of single per- sons at the 1988 General Convention as a way of raising awareness, sharing resources, building friendships, and influencing policy.

Budget Needs for 1988

Communication and Publicity

$3,600.00	Newsletters for singles' groups (expand volume by one-third), occasional notices for single parents, divorced parents
300.00	Recovery workshops, etc.
525.00	Three-color basic information brochure on the DISCOVERY ministry
750.00	Singles' schedule hot line
400.00	Special event fliers and posters for "super speakers" and other big events
1,600.00	Postage and duplicating
$7,175.00	Total

Leadership Development and Networking

$ 100.00	N.A.S.A.L. membership
1,000.00	Small group development training for "Covenant" suport and Bible study groups (three sessions at $400, $400, $200)
1,500.00	Organizational development training using Myers Briggs Indicator applications and Tavistak principles
2,500.00	Ecumenical and Episcopalian singles' network development (Kanuga and Phoenix conferences, two consultations)
150.00	Subscriptions
1,500.00	N.A.S.A.L. annual national conference in Orlando, Florida
$6,750.00	Total

Learning Programs

$3,000.00	Forty Sunday morning programs for all three singles' groups
600.00	Quarterly evening programs for all single persons
-0-	Quarterly weekend retreats (all led by ATB)
2,550.00	Special programs for single persons (open to whole parish)

$2,200.00	1. February Bible Conference, the Rev. Fred Borsch
2,500.00	2. May "Human Relations" Conference, the Rev. Roy Oswald
1,500.00	3. November "Gospel in the Workplace" conference, the Rev. Charles Price
1,500.00	4. Divorce recovery workshops
(5,150.00)	5. Income from special programs

800.00	Partial scholarships for retreat and special programs
$6,950.00	Total

Personnel

$20,000.00	Activities' Coordinator, 40 hours/week, all benefits
$24,000.00	Teacher/small group leader/counselor, 40 hours/ week including "preparation" time as well as "hands-on" time. All benefits included.
<u>1.0000.00</u>	Computer/word processor training for Activities' Coordinator
$45,000.00	Total

Evangelism

$ 1,000.00	Cost of two one-day singles' evangelism training workshops

Office Equipment and "Singles' Place" Furniture

$ 350.00	Expect donation of furniture, typewriter, filing cabinet, etc., but not telephone equipment
5,000.00	Laser printer components and training (in preparation to begin in-house printing of newsletters, etc.)
<u>2.000.00</u>	Furnishings for singles' meeting place
$ 7,350.00	Total

Athletic Equipment

$ 1,275.00	Purchase of volleyball, basketball, softball, and water sports equipment

Program Evaluation

$ 1,000.00	Costs for consultations, meetings, secretarial and clerical duties related to a review of the DISCOVERY program (probably utilizing the services of our local Center for Non-Profit Management)
$76,500.00	Grand total

Additional 1989 Goals

1. Develop a "compassionate friends" network with single volunteers, trained to reach out with care to those who have suffered a significant loss. To be developed out of the Singles' Council in concert with the Good Shepherd Program by June, 1989.
2. Develop a directory of the many types of counseling available to people in need in North Dallas, with descriptions of various approaches to problems, costs, names, and locations of practitioners, etc. To be generated out of the Singles' Council and made widely available inside and outside the parish. By September, 1989.
3. Expand on the previous year's outreach to locate and complete a major service project in conjunction with another church, institution or diocese in the Anglican Communion, preferably in Latin America, the Caribbean, or among Native Americans. The mix of differing language and culture would be built in. To be developed by the Singles' Council by June, 1989.
4. Initiate regular workshops to help those recently widowed (male and female) cope effectively with the emotional, practical, and spiritual loss of a spouse. Coordinated by the Singles' Council and the Mature Singles' Group.
5. Initiate (perhaps jointly with Youth Ministry) a "clown ministry" at St. Michael which would seek both to open people to the spiritual growth accessible through clowning and mime, and to sharing that growth with needy people in our community: hospitals, nursing homes, etc., by winter-spring of 1989.
6. Initiate (perhaps jointly with Youth and C.E.) systematic examination of the problems of alcohol and substance abuse in our community and the related over-arching patterns of spiritual/psychic disease (e.g., co-dependence) through the Singles' Council, by spring of 1989.
7. Review the DISCOVERY program with a view to consolidating things that work, shore up weaknesses, understand and let go of failures, and recommend a budget and staffing pattern for full integration into the 1990 parish operating budget.
8. Publish a monograph to be widely distributed around the church on the why, how, and wherefore of the DISCOVERY program as a resource to others, to be completed by December, 1989.

9.   Successfully begin to integrate the DISCOVERY program into the regular parish staff and operating budget, to be completed by December, 1989.

1989 Budget Goals

Communication and Publicity

$ 3,350.00	Newsletters for all singles' groups (expand volume by 1/3, savings of twenty-five percent due to laser printer)
400.00	Occasional notices
650.00	Three-color basic information on the DISCOVERY ministry
750.00	Singles' hot line
_2,000.00_	Postage and duplicating
$ 7,150.00	Total

Leadership Development and Network

$ 100.00	N.A.S.A.L. membership
1,000.00	Small group development training
1,000.00	Organizational development training (utilizing Center for Non-Profit Management)
2,500.00	Network development
1,500.00	N.A.S.A.L. annual conference
_150.00_	Subscriptions
$ 6,250.00	Total

Personnel

$21,800.00	Activities' Coordinator, full time, full benefits (calculating six percent C.O.L. plus small rise in benefit cost).
25,800.00	Teacher/small roup leader/counselor (calculating six percent C.O.L. plus small rise in benefits)

<u>1,250.00</u> Skill enhancement continuing education for both staff members

$48,850.00 Total

Learning Programs

$ 3,000.00 Forty Sunday morning programs for each Singles' group

1,200.00 Monthly evening speakers/events for all single persons

500.00 Quarterly weekend retreats (half led by ATB)

6,600.00 Special programs for all singles (and promoted to the whole parish)

$ 3,200.00 1. "How Do We Develop as Moral Persons and Persons of Faith?" Dr. James Fowler or Dr. Carol Gilligan

3,200.00 2. "Creativity and the Journey Inward," Elizabeth O'Connor

5,700.00 3. "When You Have It All and It Isn't Enough," Rabbi Harold Kuschner

2,500.00 4. Divorce recovery workshops, widowhood workshops

(8,000.00) 5. Income from special programs

<u>1,000.00</u> Partial scholarships for retreat and special programs

$ 12,300.00 Total

Compassionate Friends Network

$ 2,000.00 Start-up cost for training of pastoral visitors and administration

Evangelism

$ 500.00   Cost for one singles' evangelism workshop

Office Equipment

$ 1,200.00   Purchase of software packages to accommodate
expanding data base management needs

Athletic Equipment

$ 1,000.00   Purchase of water sports equipment

Furnishings

$ 2,500.00   Purchase of additional necessary appliances and
furniture to complete the building of "Singles'
Place." Labor again provided by singles themselves.

Service

$ 2,500.00   Start-up funds to establish relation of singles'
DISCOVERY program to an overseas mission
service setting

Program Evaluation and Preparation of Report

$ 2,000.00   Cost of preparing and publishing "the story" of the
DISCOVERY program; to be used for review of the
ministry in the parish and to be shared as a resource
with other parishes and church institutions as an
example of "how one church put together a comprehensive singles' ministry."

$86,250.00   Grand total

Why Should St. Michael Invest in This Ministry?

1. To better correlate parish priorities and programs with the population of the parish. Theologically speaking, we need to do a better job of "feeding the sheep" who happen to be in our "flock."
2. To give us the program "weapons" we need to successfully evangelize single people in north Dallas, helping this parish to maintain its "cutting edge" of new, open, and energetic and productive members.
3. To increase the stewardship of time, talent, and treasure of new and old single parishioners, thereby returning to the parish what it is investing by expanding this ministry over the next three years. We believe that increased pledges of money and talent will put this ministry "in the black" within three years.
4. Offer a uniquely episcopalian approach to singles' ministry that works carefully to integrate and not segregate people, and attends to the program principles outlined above. These principles would distinguish us from the approaches of many other churches.
5. Finally, as one of the largest Episcopal churches in the nation, we should be pioneers in moving our church at all levels to focus resources and energy on ministry to single people. We need to prod and lead our church from little interest in this ministry to an interest more in tune with the human reality of our culture.

Thank you for your consideration.

* * * * *

Personnel Specifications

I.

    A.   Job title: Activities' Coordinator for Ministry to Single Persons

    B.   Responsible to: As a member of the staff of the DISCOVERY program, the coordinator will work closely with and be responsible to the priest-in-charge of the program as designated by the rector. The priest-in-charge will define and help prioritize tasks, supervise and support the coordinator in their completion, and work with the coordinator to review regularly both functional and interpersonal aspects of their work together. The priest-in-charge will keep the rector informed in a regular way about the range of the coordinator's work and provide the rector annually with a review of that work.

C.   Definition of position: Responsible for performing secretarial, clerical, and information system functions for the DISCOVERY program, as well as other support tasks as assigned.

D.   Basic functions involved:

1)   Handle all correspondence for the program, both within and outside the parish.

2)   Insure that program newsletters are written and mailed each month in a timely fashion.

3)   Insure that newsletters and other publicity materials fully and creatively describe the various events and programs.

4)   Handle all arrangements for retreats, conferences, pleasure trips, and any other events that involve travel for single participants.

5)   Collect, deposit, and track monies collected for meals, trips, educational materials, social events, etc., from single participants.

6)   Monitor budget expenditures to insure responsible disbursement of monies on a month-to-month basis to meet program needs.

7)   Maintain current and accurate mailing lists for all active singles' groups.

8)   Take note of and insure prompt weekly attention to all single newcomers to help them feel welcome and engaged by the program.

9) Insofar as possible, stay abreast of birthdays, job changes, illnesses, and other similar crisis or transition events in the lives of single persons in the parish to facilitate pastoral attention from the priest-in-charge as well as from peers.

10) Maintain current and accurate file records of the events, programs, people, etc., of the DISCOVERY ministry to provide a record of the program's life.

11) Interact productively with other parish and professional support staff, particularly with the clergy secretary, the parish secretary, the accountant, the property manager, and the Christian education staff. Regular, mutual communication about activities of the DISCOVERY program and other parish events with the persons listed above is critical both to a healthy work environment and to the DISCOVERY program's success.

E. Personal qualities:

1) A sense of confidence both about work skills and ability to relate interpersonally.

2) A sense of personal initiative and an ability to function productively without detailed direction and supervision.

3) Good verbal communication skills and a liking for dealing with other parish staff, single parishioners, and those whose services are utilized by the program.

4) Good typing, transcribing, and word-processing skills, and an ability to increase range of experience in using information systems equipment.

5) An ability to offer and receive constructive criticism directly and sensitively in a private setting.

6) Some flexibility about scheduling (occasional evening work is required) and the ability to prioritize tasks and manage time effectively.

7)   A positive, open, and energetic spirit.

8)   A sense of empathy for single persons and a commit-
      ment to deepening the faith life of single persons in this
      community.

9)   A commitment to personal growth as a Christian and to
      being a more effective witness to the Gospel.

II.

A. Job title: Educational/Pastoral Associate

B.   Responsible to: As a member of the staff of the DISCOV-
      ERY program, the Educational/Pastoral Associate will work
      closely with and be responsible to the priest-in-charge of the
      program as designated by the rector. The priest-in-charge
      will define and help prioritize tasks, supervise, and support
      the associate in their completion and work with the associate
      to review regularly both functional and interpersonal aspects
      of their ministry together. The priest-in-charge will keep the
      rector informed about the range of the associate's work and
      provide the record annually with a review of that work.

C.   Definition of position: The Educational/Pastoral Associate
      will be responsible for preparing and conducting a variety of
      small and medium size group learning experiences, as well as
      helping to monitor and respond to pastoral problems that
      emerge both among individuals and groups that are part of the
      DISCOVERY ministry.

D. Basic functions involve:

1)   Designing, preparing for, and conducting small group
      Bible study and theological reflection groups.

2)   Preparing for and facilitating larger group discussions
      focused on theological and spiritual issues, both on
      weeknights and Sunday mornings.

3)   Help plan and lead occasional retreats for the various
      singles' groups.

4) Help plan and lead events designed to assist in the development of leadership skills and commitment among single lay participants in the DISCOVERY program.

5) Assist in the development and guidance of other small groups that focus variously on spiritual life, service to community, etc.

6) Share in the work of staying alert and responsive to individual pastoral crises and to group pastoral tensions as they occur.

7) Share in the task of supporting and guiding the various lay leadership structures of all the groups within the DIS-COVERY program to keep them open and productive.

8) Work to keep one's own life in faith dynamic by regular prayer and study.

9) Assist the priest-in-charge in the design and conduct of regular program evaluation for the DISCOVERY ministry.

10) As necessary, respond to inquiries from single persons about the various programs in order to explain the purposes of each and of the variety of study, service, and fellowship groups within the program.

E. Personal qualities and qualifications:

1) An advanced degree in theology or religious studies.

2) A sense of confidence about work skills and about ability to relate interpersonally and in an effective way.

3) A sense of personal initiative and the ability to function in a productive way without detailed direction and supervision.

4) Excellent verbal and written communication skills, and the willingness to use those skills in order to relate to

other members of the parish staff, single parishioners, and others whose services are utilized by the program.

5)   An ability to offer and receive constructive criticism directly and sensitively in private settings.

6)   Excellent educational design and communication skills as well as possessing a love of learning and the ability to share it with others.

7)   Some flexibility about schedule (occasional evening work is required), and the ability to prioritize tasks and manage time efficiently.

8)   A positive, open, and energetic spirit.

9)   A sense of empathy for single persons and a commitment to deepening the faith life of single persons in this community.

10)   A commitment to personal growth as a Christian and to being a more effective witness to the Gospel.

11)   Patience, steadiness, diplomacy, and the ability to work well with diverse people, and to function well in a complex and demanding church atmosphere.

APPENDIX FIVE

Special Liturgies
for Use with Single Populations

A. A Service of Recognition, Affirmation, and Blessing of
_____ in His/Her New Life as a Single Person

B. A Liturgy of Healing and Wholeness

C. A Liturgy for Grief and the Holidays

D. A Liturgy of Love for Valentine's Day

E. An Order for Leaving a Home

LITURGY A

A Service of Recognition, Affirmation, and Blessing of
_____ in His/Her New Life as a Single Person

(Adapted from John Westerhoff and William Willimon, *Liturgy in
Learning through the Life Cycle* [New York: Seabury Press, 1980].)

Whoever is in Christ is a new creation; the old has passed away, behold
the new has come. All this is from God, who, through Christ, reconciled
us to himself and gave us the ministry of reconciliation (2 Cor. 5:17-18).

Dear Friends: We have come together to recognize before God the
death of a marriage. We offer and present before him the pain, the anger,
the guilt, and the loneliness that have been in that death, and ask for his
mercy and redemption.

But we are here also to proclaim that death, by the grace of God, is
not only an end but also a beginning of resurrection to new life.

For in the death and resurrection of our Lord Jesus Christ, God has
revealed himself to us as one who forgives our sins, and calls us to
newness of life. As Christians, we know and proclaim that the price of
life is death.

We are witnesses, therefore, to both death and resurrection, to both
the sinfulness and forgiveness that are ours who are members one of
another in Christ.

But as members one of another, we are called to be even more than
witnesses. We are called to be a reconciling community within which
newness may be nurtured. Therefore, we now commit ourselves to
nurture and support _____ as he/she begins a new life among us.

Let us then confess our sins of the old life, both individual and
corporate, to Almighty God; knowing that if we confess our sins, he is
faithful and just to forgive them.

Have mercy upon us, most merciful Father: in your compassion
forgive us our sins, known and unknown, things done and left undone;
and so uphold us by your Spirit, that we may live and serve you in
newness of life, to the honor and glory of your Name; through Jesus
Christ our Lord. Amen.

Almighty God have mercy on you, forgive you all your sins through our Lord, Jesus Christ, strengthen you in all goodness, and by the power of the Holy Spirit keep you in eternal life. Amen.

Scripture Readings

Old Testament: Jeremiah 18:1-4
Psalm (in unison): 116:1-3, 7-8, 10-11, 15
Gospel: Matthew 7:7-11

The Homily

Declarations

_____, as you no longer live in a state of matrimony, do you freely forgive those sins committed against you by _____ in your former marriage?

A: I do forgive _____ by God's help.

Have you also sought God's forgiveness for your sins against _____?

A: By God's grace, I have.

Will you continue a concern for him/her as a fellow child of God and a brother/sister in Christ?

A: I will by God's help.

Will all of you witnessing these declarations by _____ do all in your power to uphold him/her as a single person, beloved by God?

All: We will.

Prayers

In peace, then, let us now pray to the Lord:

For the peace and unity of the Church of God, that it may be filled with truth and love, and be found without fault at the day of your coming, O Christ.

ALL: Lord, grant our prayer.

For _____ and all others who have suffered the death of their marriage, that they may accept your newness, and be blessed with your peace and freedom.

ALL: Lord, grant our prayer.

For his/her children, that they may continue to know the love of both their parents and above all know your heavenly love, so that they may also share in your recreative newness.

ALL: Lord, grant our prayer.

For those people, both present and absent, who have strengthened and supported _____ in the past, and now undertake to support his/her new life.

ALL: Lord, grant our prayer.

That in all anxieties for our future, we may continue steadfastly to put our trust in you.

ALL: Lord, grant our prayer.

For the grace to assume new responsibilities, that we may all serve you in others and love them as you love us.

ALL: Lord, grant our prayer.

In the communion of all the saints in this life and the life to come, let us commend ourselves and one another to Christ our God.

ALL: We commend ourselves to you, O Lord.

The Collect

O Lord our God, accept the fervent prayers of your people; in the multitude of your mercies, look with compassion upon us and all others who turn to you for help; for you are most gracious, O lover of souls, and to you we give glory, praise and thanks, Father, Son, and Holy Spirit, now and forever. Amen.

_____, we now recognize the end of your marriage. We recognize, affirm, and bless you as a single person among us, and we pledge you our support as you continue to seek God's help and guidance for the new life which you have undertaken in faith, through Jesus, Christ our Lord.

The Peace

The peace of the Lord be always with you.

ALL: And also with you.

Eucharist

Psalm 116

I love the Lord, because he has heard the voice of my supplication,
because he has inclined his ear to me whenever I called upon him.
The cords of death entangled me;
the grip of the grave took hold of me;
 I came to grief and sorrow.
Then, I called upon the Name of the Lord:
"O Lord, I pray you, save my life.". . .
For you have rescued my life from death,
 my eyes from tears, and my feet from stumbling.
I will walk in the presence of the Lord
 in the land of the living . . . .
How shall I repay the Lord
 for all the good things he has done for me?
I will lift up the cup of salvation
 and call upon the Name of the Lord . . . .
I will offer you the sacrifice of thanksgiving
 and call upon the Name of the Lord (RSV).

LITURGY B

A Liturgy of Healing and Wholeness
Christ Church Cathedral
Lexington, Kentucky

This service is offered on the Wednesday evening of Holy Week, signifying the death and resurrection theme of the divorce recovery work offered and allowing the participants to move into Easter with the experience of new life. (It is also offered at other times when there is sufficient need.) Participants in this service have been in divorce recovery work and believe themselves ready to take this step to conclude the divorce process and accept and bless their state of singleness. The service follows the order for the Liturgy of Healing of the Episcopal Church.

Suggested Propers might include:

The Lesson

Exodus 16:13-15 (Manna in the wilderness)
1 Kings 17:7-24 (New life)
2 Kings 5:9-14 (Suspending agendas, go with God's will)
2 Kings 20:1-5 (Prayer has been heard)
Isaiah 61:1-3 (Preach good news to the afflicted)
Acts 3:1-10 (In the name of Jesus Christ—walk)
Romans 8:18-23 (Set free from struggles)
Romans 8:31-39 (Nothing separates us from the love of God)
2 Corinthians 1:3-5 (God comforts our afflictions)
Colossians 1:11-20 (God strengthens with all power)
James 5:13-16 (Are you suffering? Pray)

The Gospel

Matthew 26:36-39 (Jesus in Gethsemane)
John 5:1-9 (Do you want to be healed?)
John 6:47-51 (I am the bread of life)

The Homily

(The celebrant should know something about the community to which he/she will minister and go to the scriptures accordingly.)

(Summary) The general rule for this homily is "hurt a little, heal a little, hope a little." The first part of the homily involves the pain of the first step of healing—the cleaning out of the wound. Healing cannot occur if the individual is not aware of the injury. The pain of the divorce experience is dealt with honestly—the broken relationships, relationships which have died, relationships which have been abusive and destructive, unresolved anger, difficult forgiveness, the struggle of trying to live single, be a single parent, broken dreams, lost hopes. Depending on the particular style of the homilist and the group and setting, these issues may be stated directly, or more symbolically.

Part 2 of the homily reminds us that healing is what God wants, is God's business, and his way with us. Reflecting on scripture, we learn that God's response to suffering is not to ignore it, or to punish us, but to say let me join you in your suffering; I have joined you; I am with you in that suffering. Out of that union comes all of the possibility of God's promises, leading into the theme of hope for Part 3 of the homily. Behold, I make all things new. The homilist will express this resurrection and transfiguration theme in ways which have been real to him/her.

The Healing

The celebrant invites the participants to come to the altar rail to receive the sacrament of healing, explaining that they will each have an opportunity to express to him/her (the celebrant) what it is they wish to offer up for healing—specific names of persons, actions, attitudes, etc.—and that they will be signed with the sign of the cross and receive the laying on of hands as the prayer for healing is individually said.

The celebrant listens with the heart, conscious of the journey these individuals have made in their divorce recovery work, and in the first parts of this service, as the celebrant helps them offer their pain to God. He/she speaks from the heart when praying with (not for) the healing, remembering the role of the shaman is to join the person and speak to God with them, on their behalf. The sign of the cross is made on the forehead as the person is anointed with oil. They receive the laying on of hands as the celebrant offers individual prayers to strengthen, sustain, open their hearts, etc.

Hymn

"I come with joy to meet my Lord, forgiven, loved and free" (#304),
The Episcopal Hymnal 1982

The Eucharist

Hymn

"Amazing Grace"

The Blessing and Dismissal

At the conclusion of the service, the participants all share a common
meal in celebration of their new life.

Optional Prayers

Heavenly Father, I commit to you the union that once was made in your
name, and my partner in that union. With your help, I forgive those sins
which were committed against me, and I forgive myself for those sins
which I committed. Amen.

Dear Lord, please bless my children, whose hearts were torn by this
division in their lives, and who must live in this division. Help them to
know the love of both their father and their mother, and, above all, bring
them to know the fullness of the love of you, their heavenly Father.
Amen.

Father, I also ask your blessing upon all those friends and special
helpers who have unstintingly given to me of their strength, their faith,
and their love in my time of sorrow and pain, and who go with me into
my new life. Amen.

Dear Lord God, I ask your strength and guidance as I release the life
that I once knew, and turn toward the new life which is now mine. Help
me to remember those things which I have learned in the wilderness of
despair, and offer now to you, that I may, in my new life, be a witness to
your unfailing love, which sustains me now and forever. Amen.

Heavenly Father, I come before you as you created me, one person,

whole and unique in your eyes. I offer you my life to use as you would deem best for me, and for your greater purpose in the community to which you call me, and in the world. Thank you for the healing and wholeness you have brought to my life, and, above all, for the knowledge that I am worthy in your eyes, and sustained by your love.
Amen.

LITURGY C

A Liturgy for Grief and the Holidays
Christ Church Cathedral
Lexington, Kentucky

While this service originated in a series of classes offered by Singles'
Ministries, it is open to the parish and to the community. Participants in
the service may be grieving the loss of spouse through death or divorce,
the loss of family or a family member, loss of body part, loss of home,
loss of job, loss of pet, loss of a dream. Some griefs may be quite recent,
while others are recurring griefs which may surface during the holiday
season.

In sessions 1 and 2 of a series of classes called Grief and the Holidays, participants have experienced confession in "It's the Holidays and I
Don't Feel Like Celebrating," and further preparation during "Others
Have Walked This Way Before." This service is the concluding hour of
session 3, called "In Sacrament and Symbol, We Remember." Its intention is to help and support those who are grieving by allowing them a
way to include that grief in their holiday.

Format

Participants sit in a circle. The table is in the center of the circle. The
bread and wine are on the table; there is also a nonflammable tray to
receive the votive candles. Each participant has a votive candle(s)
available.

This service is based on Rite Three from *The Book of Common
Prayer*. The people and priest gather in the name of the lord.

LEADER: Dear friends, we are gathered here tonight to share our grief
and pain as we partake of the Sacrament of the Body and Blood of the
Lord Jesus Christ. In these past weeks, we have come to this place to
recognize that as the world around us is anticipating and moving toward
the holiday season, our hearts are burdened with pain and burdened with
guilt because we feel this pain in a season of joy. So we seek this place
of love and light—a haven where we can give ourselves permission to

feel our grief, our anger, our pain, and our fear—and to know others who carry such burdens, in seeming contradiction to this approaching season. Here we have spoken of our loves and losses; we have wept; we have shared; we have even laughed.

We know that grieving is a part of living, and that you grieved and suffered.

There is in Tibetan Buddhist ritual: a story of a bowl. We each carry with us such a bowl. It contains within it all of our bitterness, hardness, and disillusionment. We hold it in front of us. We can either pour the contents of the bowl forward and allow the whole resentful mess to flow away from us, or we can tip it the other way and pour it into ourselves allowing the poison to infect our blood. Alan Jones, in his book *Journey into Christ*, says,

> For the one who, in that split second is given the grace to pour the blood of bitterness onto the receiving earth and not into himself, there is the beginning of the recognition of the creative love in the deep but dazzling darkness of God. He begins to see God at work, summoning him to a joy which makes all of the happiness he has hitherto known as nothing.

Psalm 23

The Gospel

Optional Homily or Reading

The Prayers of the People

Father, I come to you this day bearing the pain of great loss—loss made more poignant in the joy and anticipation around me. Help me to know the eternal truth and joy beneath the externals, that I may come to the birth of your son with heart open and ready to receive this great gift.

ALL: Lord, hear our prayer.

Lord God, into your hands I give the anger, sadness, envy, bitterness, resentment, and the pain which seem too great for me to bear, and which come unbidden and unwanted, even in the face of this season of joy. Cleanse me, Father, and make me whole.

ALL: Lord, hear our prayer.

Father, I thank you for the gift of memories and pray that you will help me cherish those memories without worshiping them; to release those which cause pain and discomfort to anyone, or which prevent my acceptance of your healing power in my life.

ALL: Lord, hear our prayer.

Dear Lord, I offer special thanks for friends and loved ones who have been a comfort and support to me in this time of bereavement and are a continuing blessing in my life. I ask your particular blessing upon them now.

ALL: Lord, hear our prayer.

Father, help me to forgive those things which have been done or left undone which have brought me pain. Especially help me forgive myself for those things which I regret.

ALL: Lord, hear our prayer.

Lord, thank you for your loving kindness in bringing moments which show me that there is light after darkness, hope after despair, faith after doubt, safety after fear, and, always, your holy presence to bring these truths to me, if I will but ask.

ALL: Lord, hear our prayer.

Especially, Father *(individual intercessions and thanksgivings are spoken). (Conclude with prayers for all sufferers, and others from forms "Prayers of the People,"* The Book of Common Prayer, *pp. 383-393.)*

Absolution

The Peace

Preparation of Table

Offering of the Light

LEADER: Dear friends, we have each brought with us to this service a special memory, which has once brought us joy and now fills us with pain, so that it is difficult to see the light of this season. As we prepare our hearts to receive the light of Jesus, we offer this gift of candles, to remind us of his light in our darkness.

(Light candle 1) The first light is the light of courage—to face each day and its tasks.

(Light candle 2) The second light is the candle of tears, those healing agents which we have been promised in scripture that God knows, holds, and consoles.

(Light candle 3) The third light is the light of strength, which God alone provides, and which we receive in our weakness and vulnerability.

(Light candle 4) The fourth light is the light of hope, which is brought into the world again each Christmas, to live in our hearts.

(Leader says to participants) At this time, you may wish to light another candle to symbolize someone or something in your heart. As you place that bright light upon the altar, may you trust all that it represents to our heavenly Father.

The Holy Eucharist

The prayer of consecration is offered by the priest.
The people serve each other in a circle, using the words:
"The Body of Christ, the Bread of Heaven"
"The Blood of Christ, the Cup of Salvation."

Thanksgiving and Dismissal

Optional Hymn

LITURGY D

A Liturgy of Love for Valentine's Day
as used at the University Episcopal Center
University of Minnesota

Following the Order for the Holy Eucharist, Rite Two from *The Book of Common Prayer*

Collect

Easter 6 Collect: O God, you have prepared for those who love you such good things as surpass our understanding. Pour into our hearts such love towards you, that we, loving you in all things and above all things, may obtain your promises, which exceed all that we can desire; through Jesus Christ our Lord, who lives and reigns with you and the Holy Spirit, one God, forever and ever. Amen.

or

Collect of the Incarnation: O God, who wonderfully created, and yet more wonderfully restored, the dignity of human nature; grant that we may share the divine life of him who humbled himself to share our humanity, your Son Jesus Christ; who lives and reigns with you, in the unity of the Holy Spirit, one God, forever and ever. Amen.

or

O God of love, whose love is stronger than the arrows of cupid, whose endurance is more than a box of candy or flowers, be present with us and draw us into a relationship with you and one another, that in our love we may reflect your glorious image; through Jesus Christ our Savior. Amen.

The Lessons
    1 Corinthians 13
    John 3:16

Hymns

"God is love, and where true love is, God is present there"
(#577), *The Episcopal Hymnal 1982*

"What wondrous love is this?"
(#439), *The Episcopal Hymnal 1982*

Sermon/Reflection

(Summary) We acknowledge the day as a day when couples and cou-
pling are emphasized in the world, and how painful it often is for singles
to live through this day. We remind people that biblical history is not a
"couple's history," but, rather, a history of people—tribes and communities. We remind people that the one who most represents God's love
does not call us into coupledom, but rather into a relationship with God
and with one another. While that might mean for some a relationship of
love, it may mean for others many relationships expressing love in
community. "Love one another" is not simply a valentine slogan, but a
way of living in the world. In a reflection, we invite persons to reflect on
some ways they have been loved and how they have given love in their
lives, which usually elicits much conversation.

If there is time, we read either 1 Corinthians or the Gospel again,
and invite people to love one another as a community gathered in love to
celebrate their lives in the Eucharist.

We then pray for the world for all those who are alone and lonely,
for the ill, etc. Afterwards, we have a Valentine's Day party with re-
freshments and ask people to sign or write a valentine card to someone
who is homebound or grieving, someone in prison, or someone in a
nursing home. (We usually have several names and addresses of persons
with brief descriptions of the situation available.) In the past, we have
sent valentines to political prisoners (via Amnesty International), to
military folk who are conscientious objectors imprisoned for their beliefs
and refusal to fight, to persons in homeless shelters (we fill out a large
number of them and deliver them for the evening meal, signing the cards
with first names only), etc.

LITURGY E

An Order for Leaving a Home

This Order follows the Order for Daily Devotions for Individuals and Families, *The Book of Common Prayer*, p. 136.

A minister, priest, or lay person shall officiate.

Psalm

Psalm 30 (suggested)

Reading

2 Corinthians 4:5-6

The Collect

O God, you have prepared for those who love you such good things as surpass our understanding; pour into our hearts such love towards you, that we, loving you in all things and above all things, may obtain your promises, which exceed all that we can desire, through Jesus Christ our Lord, who lives and reigns with you and the Holy Spirit, one God, forever and ever. Amen.

Special Prayers

O God, you have blessed me with the gift of this home, and with the friends and loved ones who have joined me in knowing its graces.

ALL: Thank you, Lord.

You have given me the blessing of laughter and good times within these walls.

ALL: Thank you, Lord.

You have been with me in times of darkness and pain, as you promised.

ALL: Thank you, Lord.

You have given me the gift of memory, that I may recall with joy and strength, to go forward in my life, as you have called me now to do.

ALL: Thank you, Lord.

Father, I know that you are the castle in which I dwell most safely; my strong rock, and my stronghold. In this earthly home, and in whatever earthly homes I may live, help me to remember these truths, that I may know you are ever with me, and I in you. Amen.

Homily or Special Words and/or Ceremony

(Summary) The person for whom this service is being held may wish to have a short ritual here, which says goodbye to the home, and moves the worshipers into the new life. For example, the dining room table is symbolically removed and becomes the first piece of furniture carried together to a waiting van; or a special poem or reading might be given. This offers an opportunity for the individual to incorporate those persons, words, or actions which seem to be appropriate and helpful ways of bringing closure to one way of life and entering another. It would also be appropriate to celebrate the Eucharist at this point in the service, or to include here a community meal or picnic, with the previous part of the Order serving as the Grace before the shared meal, and the concluding portion as the blessing and dismissal.

The Lord's Prayer

(It is also appropriate to include other intercessions, prayers of thanksgiving, the General Thanksgiving.)

Closing Prayer

We thank you, Lord, that you go with us now, as you have gone with your children through the ages. In the strength of your love, and the power of the Holy Spirit, we go forth. Amen.

ALL: Thanks be to God.

NOTES

Chapter 1

1. Cited in James Solheim, "Episcopal Church Showing Signs of Growth," Episcopal News Service, March 20, 1992.

2. Carolyn Koons and M. J. Anthony, *Single Adult Passages: Uncharted Territory* (Grand Rapids, MI: Baker Books, 1991), 36.

3. Carolyn Koons, "Single Adult Passages: A Unique Look," audio taped address, Montreat, NC (July 1991). Distributed by National Single Leaders Consortium.

4. Janet Fishburn, *Confronting the Idolatry of Family: A New Vision for the Household of God* (Nashville: Abingon Press, 1991), 32.

5. Ibid., 31.

6. Ibid., 32.

Chapter 3

1. Cited in Carolyn Koons and M. J. Anthony, *Single Adult Passages: Uncharted Territory* (Grand Rapids, MI.: Baker Books, 1991), 207.

2. John Shelby Spong, *Living in Sin? A Bishop Rethinks Human Sexuality* (San Francisco: Harper & Row, 1988), 188.

3. Ibid., 190.

4. Ibid., 92.

5. John Westerhoff and William Willimon, *Liturgy in Learning through the Life Cycle* (New York: Seabury Press, 1980), 124-131.

6. Available from Serendipity House, Box 1012, Littleton, CO 80160.

Chapter 4

1. Emmalou Benignus, "One Is a Whole Number," keynote address, Solo Flight Conference, Kanuga Conference Center, Hendersonville, NC (November 1991).

2. Susan Muto, "Claiming Singleness as God's Gift and Call," audio taped address.

3. Alla Renee Campbell, *Life Is Goodbye, Life Is Hello* (Minneapolis: CompCare, 1992).

4. Harold Ivan Smith, "Single Adult Ministries and Their Taboo Topic of Death," address, National Single Leaders Consortium, Orlando, FL (May 1991).

5. Carole George and Marcia Lawrence, in *The Messenger* (December 1991).

6. Carolyn Koons and M. J. Anthony, *Single Adult Passages; Uncharted Territory* (Grand Rapids, MI, 1991), 206.

Chapter 5

1. Robert Raymond, keynote address, Presbyterian Singles' Conference, Montreat, NC (July 1, 1991). Preferred Futures Now, Edena, MN.

2. *The Book of Common Prayer* (New York: Seabury Press, 1979), 339, emphasis added.

Resources for Single Adult Ministry

Brown, Raymond Kay. *Reach Out to Singles*. Philadelphia: The Westminster Press, 1979.

Christoff, Nicholas B. *Saturday Night, Sunday Morning: Singles and the Church*. San Francisco: Harper & Row, 1980.

Fagerstrom, Douglas L., ed. *Singles' Ministry Handbook*. Wheaton, IL: Victor Books, 1989.

___. *Developing Single Adult Ministry. Singles' Ministry Handbook*. Wheaton, IL: Victor Books, forthcoming early 1993.

___. *Counseling Single Adults*. Grand Rapids, MI: Baker Books, forthcoming 1993.

Fishburn, Janet. *Confronting the Idolatry of Family: A New Vision for the Household of God*. Nashville: Abingdon Press, 1991.

Hershey, Terry, Karen Butler, Richard Hurst. *Giving the Ministry Away: Empowering SIngle Adults for Effective Leadership*. Colorado Springs, CO: Navpress, 1992.

Jones, Jerry, ed. *Single Adult Ministry*. Colorado Springs, CO: Navpress, 1992.

Lyon, William. *A Pew for One, Please: The Church and the Single Person*. New York: Seabury Press, 1977.

Reed, Bobbie. *Single on Sunday: A Manual for Successful Single Adult Ministries*. St. Louis: Concordia Publishing House, 1979.

Vogelsang, John, Ph.D., ed. *Singleness and Community: Toward the Whole People of God*. Minneapolis: Lutheran-Episcopal Center, forthcoming 1992.

General Reading to Expand Knowledge of Singleness

Collier-Slone, Kay, Ph.D. *Launchings for the Solo Flight* (essays). Box
    24041, Lexington, KY: Life Force Press, 1991.
Edwards, Marie, and Eleanor Hoover. *The Challenge of Being Single.*
    New York: New American Library, 1975.
Koons, Carolyn, and M. J. Anthony. *Single Adult Passages: Uncharted
    Territory.* Grand Rapids: Baker Book House, 1991.
Miller, Keith, and Andrea Wells Miller. *The Single Experience.* Waco,
    TX: Word Books, 1981.
Nichols, J. Randall. *Ending Marriage, Keeping Faith.* New York:
    Crossroad, 1991.
Smith, Harold Ivan. *Forty-something and Single.* Wheaton, IL: Victor
    Books, 1991.
____. *Singles Ask.* Minneapolis: Augsburg Publishing House, 1988.
____. *Single and Feeling Good.* Nashville: Abingdon Press, 1988.
Streeter, Carole Sanderson. *Reflections for Women Alone.* Wheaton, IL:
    Victor Books, 1987.

Readings on Divorce/Divorce Recovery

Bernard and Hackney. *Untying the Knot.* Minneapolis: Winston Press,
    1983.
Bridges, William. *Transitions: Making Sense of Life's Changes.*
    Reading, MA: Addison-Wesley, 1980.
Colgroave, Bloomfield, and Peter McWilliams. *How to Survive the Loss
    of a Love.* New York: Bantam Books, 1981.
Ebaugh, Helen Rose Fuchs. *Become an Ex: The Process of Role Exit.*
    Chicago: The University of Chicago Press, 1988.
Fintushel, N., and N. Hillard, Ph.D. *A Grief Out of Season.* Boston:
    Little, Brown and Company, 1992.
Johnson, Stephen M., Ph.D. *First-Person Singular: Living the Good
    Life Alone.* New York: Signet Books, 1977.
Krantzler, Mel. *Creative Divorce.* New York: Signet Books, 1974.
Napolitane, Catherine, and Victoria Pellegrino. *Living and Loving after
    Divorce.* New York: Signet Books, 1977.
Patton, John. *Is Human Forgiveness Possible?* Nashville: Abingdon
    Press, 1985.

Schuller, Robert A. *Getting through the Going-Through Stage.* Nashville: Thomas Nelson Publishers, 1986.

Smedes, Lewis B. *Forgive and Forget: Healing the Hurts You Don't Deserve.* San Francisco: Harper & Row, 1984.

Smith, Harold Ivan. *I Wish Someone Understood My Divorce.* Minneapolis: Augsburg Publishing House, 1984.

Smoke, Jim. *Growing through Divorce.* New York: Bantam Books, 1978.

Streeter, Carole Anderson. *Finding Your Place after Divorce: How Women Can Find Healing.* Grand Rapids: Zondervan, 1986.

Trafford, Abigail. *Crazy Time: Surviving Divorce.* New York: Bantam Books, 1984.

Triere, Lynette, and Richard Peacock. *Learning to Leave.* New York: Warner Books, 1982.

Readings on Children of Divorce

Berger, Stuart, M.D. *Divorce without Victims: Helping Children through Divorce with a Minimum of Pain and Trauma.* New York: Signet Books, 1986.

Berman Claire. *A Hole in My Heart: Adult Children of Divorce Speak Out.* New York: Simon and Schuster, 1991.

Bienefeld, Florence, Ph.D. *Helping Your Child Succeed after Divorce.* Claremont, Calif.: Hunter House Publishers, 1987.

Diamond, Susan Arnsberg. *Helping Children of Divorce.* New York: Schocken Books, 1985.

Fassel, Diane. *Growing Up Divorced.* New York: Pocket Books, 1991.

Kline, Kris, and Stephen Pew, Ph.D. *For the Sake of the Children. How to Share Your Children with Your Ex-spouse in Spite of Your Anger.* Rocking, PA: Prima Publishing, 1992.

Ricci, Isolina. *Mom's House, Dad's House: Healing the Hurts.* Kansas City, MO.: Beacon Hill Press, 1980.

Smith, Harold Ivan. *Help for Parents of a Divorced Son or Daughter.* St. Louis: Concordia Publishing House, 1981.

Virtue, Doreen. *My Kids Don't Live with Me Anymore: Coping with the Custody Crisis.* Minneapolis: CompCare Publications, 1988.

Wallerstein, Judith S., and Sandra Blakeslee. *Second Chances: Men, Women and Children a Decade after Divorce. Who Wins, Who Loses, and Why.* New York: Ticknor and Fields, 1989.

Readings on Grief Recovery

Bozarth, Alla Renee. *Life Is Goodbye, Life Is Hello.* Minneapolis: CompCare Publications, 1992.

Deits, B. *Life after Loss.* Tucson, AZ: Fisher Books, 1988.

L'Engle, Madeleine. *Two-Part Invention.* New York: Farrar, Straus & Giroux, 1988.

Oates, Wayne. *Your Particular Grief.* Philadelphia: The Westminster Press, 1981.

Shaw, Luci. *God in the Dark: Through Grief and Beyond.* Grand Rapids: Zondervan Books, 1990.

Stearns, A. K. *Living through Personal Loss.* New York: Ballantine Books, 1984.

Readings on Loneliness

Bernikow, Louise. *Alone in America.* New York: Harper & Row, 1986.

Kottler, Jeffrey, Ph.D. *Private Moments, Secret Selves: Enriching Our Time Alone.* New York: Ballantine Books, 1990.

Moustakis, Clark, Ph.D. *Loneliness.* Englewood, NJ: Prentice Hall, 1977.

Muto, Susan. *Celebrating the Single Life: A Spirituality for Single Persons in Today's World.* Garden City, NY: Doubleday and Company, Inc., 1982.

Readings on Relationships and Remarriage

Kelly, Kevin T. *Divorce and Second Marriage: Facing the Challenge.* New York: Seabury Press, 1983.

Krantzler, Mel. *Learning to Love Again.* New York: Bantam Books, 1977.

Smoke, Jim. *Growing in Remarriage.* Old Tappan, NJ: Fleming H. Revell, 1990.

Stuart, Richard B., and Barbara Jacobson. *Second Marriage.* New York: W. W. Norton and Company, 1985.

The Alban Institute:
an invitation to membership

The Alban Institute, begun in 1979, believes that the congregation is essential to the task of equipping the people of God to minister in the church and the world. A multi-denominational membership organization, the Institute provides on-site training, educational programs, consulting, research, and publishing for hundreds of churches across the country.

The Alban Institute invites you to be a member of this partnership of laity, clergy, and executives—a partnership that brings together people who are raising important questions about congregational life and people who are trying new solutions, making new discoveries, finding a new way of getting clear about the task of ministry. The Institute exists to provide you with the kinds of information and resources you need to support your ministries.

Join us now and enjoy these benefits:

CONGREGATIONS, The Alban Journal, a highly respected journal published six times a year, to keep you up to date on current issues and trends.

Inside Information, Alban's quarterly newsletter, keeps you informed about research and other happenings around Alban. Available to members only.

Publications Discounts:

☐ 15% for Individual, Retired Clergy, and Seminarian Members
☐ 25% for Congregational Members
☐ 40% for Judicatory and Seminary Executive Members

Discounts on Training and Education Events

Write our Membership Department at the address below or call us at (202) 244-7320 for more information about how to join The Alban Institute's growing membership, particularly about Congregational Membership in which 12 designated persons receive all benefits of membership.

The Alban Institute, Inc.
4125 Nebraska Avenue, NW
Washington, DC 20016